D0422407

IN PRAISE OF BLAME

IN PRAISE OF BLAME

George Sher

WARNER MEMORIAL LIBRARY
EASTERN UNIVERSITY
ST. DAVIDS, PA 19087-3696

OXFORD
UNIVERSITY PRESS

2006

1-9-7

BJ 1535 .F3 S54 2005
Sher, George.
In praise of blame

OXFORD
UNIVERSITY PRESS

Oxford University Press, Inc., publishes works that further
Oxford University's objective of excellence
in research, scholarship, and education.

Oxford   New York
Auckland   Cape Town   Dar es Salaam   Hong Kong   Karachi
Kuala Lumpur   Madrid   Melbourne   Mexico City   Nairobi
New Delhi   Shanghai   Taipei   Toronto

With offices in
Argentina   Austria   Brazil   Chile   Czech Republic   France   Greece
Guatemala   Hungary   Italy   Japan   Poland   Portugal   Singapore
South Korea   Switzerland   Thailand   Turkey   Ukraine   Vietnam

Copyright © 2006 by Oxford University Press, Inc.

Published by Oxford University Press, Inc.
198 Madison Avenue, New York, New York 10016

www.oup.com

Oxford is a registered trademark of Oxford University Press.

All rights reserved. No part of this publication may be reproduced,
stored in a retrieval system, or transmitted, in any form or by any means,
electronic, mechanical, photocopying, recording, or otherwise,
without prior permission of Oxford University Press.

Library of Congress Cataloging-in-Publication Data
Sher, George.
In praise of blame/George Sher.
p. cm.
Includes bibliographical references and index.
ISBN-13 978-0-19-518742-7
ISBN 0-19-518742-3
1. Faultfinding.   2. Blame.   3. Conduct of life.   I. Title.
BJ1535.F3S54   2005
179'.8—dc22   2005040635

1   3   5   7   9   8   6   4   2

Printed in the United States of America
on acid-free paper

For Emily, Sally, and Joe

PREFACE

Blame is as common as water and as transparent to the gaze. We all know what it is but we cannot explain what we know by describing the experience. Often, there is no experience to describe. We also cannot explain what we know by specifying blame's purpose, since genuine blame is always impotent because always after the fact. Given its ubiquity, its elusiveness, and its evident moral importance, we might expect philosophers to have scrutinized blame carefully.

But, strikingly, they have not. The 2003 edition of *The Philosopher's Index*, which publishes abstracts of all the books and articles that appear on each topic in philosophy within a given year, contains 114 entries on responsibility and 24 on punishment but only 2 on blame. I am not sure why blame has not received more attention, but whatever the explanation, the absence of a significant literature on the topic is really quite remarkable.

Philosophers neglect blame, but are as a group not actively hostile toward it. By contrast, those in the social sciences and the "helping professions" have displayed a fair amount of hostility. According to many in these fields, blame is ugly and destructive—a grim anachronism we would all be better off without. Instead of being "judgmental," we are told to react to wrongdoing by "putting it behind us"; instead of condemning misbehavior, we are urged to understand its "root causes";

instead of dwelling on what cannot be changed, we are enjoined to concentrate on "healing."

As might be expected in a society dominated by the therapeutic ethos, this antipathy to blame has found its way into the wider culture. Consider, for example, the following composite passage from a book entitled *A Guide to Rational Living*—a work that, according to its cover, has sold a million and a half copies:

> We can actually put the essence of neurosis in a single word: blaming—or damning. . . . To damn others means you make yourself angry or hostile toward them. Feelings of anger reflect your grandiosity. . . . Blaming yourself or others not only leads to anger, as just noted, but to many unpleasant consequences of rage. . . . Fistfights, duels, torture, rape, wars—in fact, virtually every violent aspect of people's inhumanity to people that you can think of—have resulted from our grandiosely damning others whose actions we (perhaps rightly) consider wrong. And just as two wrongs don't make a right, rage against offenders is probably the worst way to try to correct them.[1]

Although the writing is overwrought, the actual message of the passage is not atypical. For further illustration of the idea that blame is toxic, the reader is invited to consult the self-help section of any bookstore.

My aim here is to remedy the neglect of philosophers while showing the antagonism of the therapeutically oriented to be misplaced. Blame, I will argue, should be neither ignored nor deplored. One reason to take it seriously is that it raises a host of deep analytical and normative problems, many of which have not even been noticed, let alone resolved, by philosophers. A further reason, more important yet, is that the concept of blameworthiness, in which a reference to blame is embedded, is central to our moral thought. We commonly distinguish between the question of whether what someone did was wrong and the question of whether, if the act was wrong, the agent is blameworthy for performing it; and we commonly take the second question to be just as important as the first. It is, indeed, largely because determinism calls

---

1. Albert Ellis and Robert A. Harper, *A Guide to Rational Living*, 3rd ed. (North Hollywood, Calif.: Wilshire Book Company, 1997), 127, 129–30.

into question our ability to view wrongdoers as blameworthy that we take its threats to freedom and responsibility as seriously as we do. Given the importance that we attach to judgments of blameworthiness, it is natural to wonder what those judgments involve. We are, however, unlikely to understand this if we do not understand what those whom we take to be blameworthy are thought to be worthy of.

As should be clear, the phenomenon that interests me is *moral* blame. This is not the only form of blame. We do something different when we blame the collapse of a bridge on rusted support beams or low voter turnout on an unexpected rainstorm. When we blame the rust or the rainstorm, we are saying only that it was an especially important (because especially salient or manipulable) member of the total set of conditions and events that led to the relevant bad outcome. Such assertions attribute causality but involve no moral criticism. By contrast, when we blame someone for breaking his promise, we do not imply that he did any harm but we do imply that his act was morally defective. In what follows, I will confine my attention to blame of this second sort.[2]

When philosophers have discussed blame at all, they have generally considered it only as a member of a larger family of reactions—one that also includes praise, punishment, and reward—that determinism threatens *en bloc*. Because the free will debate looms so large, the philosopher's eye is constantly drawn to it. My strategy here will be to turn my gaze in another direction to gain a clearer view of what usually goes unnoticed. Instead of confronting the threat of determinism, I will simply assume that some actual or possible version of compatibilism is capable of defusing it. Although I will, of course, consider the views of contributors to the free will debate, incompatibilist as well as

2. Although the distinction between moral and nonmoral blame is clear enough in the polar cases, there is an intermediate type of case that combines elements of each. The type of case I am thinking of is one in which we blame a lazy student for his bad grades or a reckless driver for his own injuries. What makes this type of case intermediate is that it involves a form of criticism—namely, a charge of insufficient prudence—that is partly like, but partly unlike, moral criticism. I hereby take note of, but do not intend to pursue, the question of how much of what can be said about moral blame can also be said about this intermediate form of blame.

compatibilist, I will do so only when, and only to the extent that, they are relevant to blame in particular.

While writing this book I incurred debts to various individuals and institutions, and I am pleased to acknowledge them here. I am grateful to Baruch Brody, Anne Farber, Donald Morrison, and David Phillips for their helpful comments on material that eventually found its way into the manuscript. I have also benefited from discussion with the members of various audiences to whom I presented parts of the book, and with the participants in the moral psychology seminar that I taught in the fall semester of 2004 at Rice University. I am grateful to Rice University itself for granting me a research leave in 2000–01 and to the National Endowment for the Humanities for providing part of the funding for that leave. Some of the material that appears in chapter 2 was originally published in *Philosophy and Phenomenological Research*, while an earlier version of chapter 4 appeared in *Nous*. I thank both journals for permission to reprint that material here.

I am especially pleased to acknowledge two further debts. One is to my former colleague Nomy Arpaly, with whom I have discussed these topics at length and who read and commented on a number of drafts of this manuscript. Her incisive suggestions have been invaluable in crystallizing my thinking and have greatly improved the final product. The other debt, my greatest, is to my wife Emily Fox Gordon, who combines literary perfect pitch with a shrewd native philosophical sensibility. She has been a staunch and unyielding ally in the long struggle to bring language and thought together. I thank her once again for helping to make the writing life a joy.

CONTENTS

IN PRAISE OF BLAME

ONE

INTRODUCTION

EVER SINCE THE PUBLICATION OF P. F. STRAWSON'S CLASSIC ESSAY "FREEDOM and Resentment" in 1962,[1] philosophers have been aware that our lives would be profoundly altered if we were to relinquish what Strawson called the "reactive attitudes"—a class of responses to good will or its absence in ourselves or others that includes both various blame-related attitudes such as resentment, indignation, guilt, and forgiveness, and various other attitudes including gratitude, love, and hurt feelings. Strawson's own view was that abandoning the reactive attitudes would immeasurably impoverish our interpersonal lives, but that their disappearance is not something we need to worry about because it is, for practical purposes, an impossibility. I am not sure whether Strawson was right to make the second claim—he may have been confusing the limits of the practically possible with those of the currently conceivable—but he clearly was right in making the first. To convey an initial sense of the role that blame plays in our lives, I want to follow Strawson in asking how its disappearance would alter them.

The alteration would not necessarily be as great as the one Strawson envisioned. His question was what our interaction with others

---

1. P. F. Strawson, "Freedom and Resentment," in *Free Will*, ed. Derk Pereboom (Indianapolis, Ind.: Hackett, 1997), 119–42.

would be like if we abandoned the reactive attitudes en masse; and his answer was that we would then be thrown back on what he called the objective attitude:

> To adopt the objective attitude to another human being is to see him, perhaps, as an object of social policy; as a subject for what, in a wide range of sense, might be called treatment; as something certainly to be taken account, perhaps precautionary account, of; to be managed or handled or cured or trained; perhaps simply to be avoided . . . it cannot include the range of reactive feelings and attitudes which belong to involvement or participation with others in inter-personal human relationships; it cannot include resentment, gratitude, forgiveness, anger, or the sort of love which two adults can sometimes be said to feel reciprocally, for each other.[2]

The idea that our social relations might thus come to lack all mutuality is so obviously alien and repellant as to require no comment.

Yet even if Strawson is right to see the disappearance of mutuality as the inevitable outcome of the abandonment of all reactive attitudes, it would pretty clearly not be the inevitable outcome of a more selective shift away from blame and cognate attitudes such as resentment, indignation, and guilt. The absence of blame would indeed mean that we could not forgive anyone, but that is simply because forgiving presupposes blame. There is, as far as I can see, no comparable reason to expect that the disappearance of blame would make it impossible to like or love some people while disliking or hating others, to have both friends and enemies, to admire accomplishment while deploring slackness and missed opportunities, to be gratified when others display good will toward us and disappointed when they do not, and so on. The idea that our social relations might someday all take this form is far less alien and repellant than the wholesale objectification that Strawson envisions.

Less alien and repellant, perhaps, but alien and repellant still; and to see why, we need only ask how someone who rejected blame *would* be able to respond to behavior that was malicious, evil, or simply wrong.

---

2. Strawson, "Freedom and Resentment," 126–27.

In an interesting discussion of the modes of interaction that would remain legitimate if determinism were to deprive all agents of responsibility, Derk Pereboom has suggested that

> instead of blaming people, the determinist might appeal to the practice of moral admonishment and encouragement. One might, for example, explain to an offender that what he did was wrong, and then encourage him to refrain from performing similar actions in the future. One need not, in addition, blame him for what he has done. The hard determinist can maintain that by admonishing and encouraging a wrongdoer one might communicate a sense of what is right, and a respect for persons, and that these attitudes can lead to salutary change.[3]

Along similar lines, Pereboom writes that a hard determinist who was wronged by a friend or lover

> would resist anger, blame, and resentment, but she would not be exempt from pain and unhappiness upon being wronged. She might, if wronged, admonish, disregard the wrongdoing, or terminate the relationship.[4]

In these remarkable passages, Pereboom vividly, if unwittingly, illustrates just how strange—I am tempted to say "inhuman"—a world without blame would be.

The strangeness, indeed, is present at several levels. It is, first, no accident that Pereboom's tone is one of bland, dissociated innocence; for his world without blame, though not without wrongdoing, is devoid of true—that is, freely chosen—evil. Not coincidentally, it is also a world in which human motivation does not conform to familiar patterns. In our actual experience, there is not only nothing to be gained by solemnly informing a carjacker or rapist that he has violated the

---

3. Derk Pereboom, "Determinism *Al Dente*," in *Free Will*, 260.

4. Ibid., 271. For further development of Pereboom's ideas about how we might respond to wrongdoing if we ceased to blame wrongdoers, see Derk Pereboom, *Living Without Free Will* (Cambridge: Cambridge University Press, 2001). For related discussion, see Ted Honderich, *A Theory of Determinism: The Mind, Neuroscience, and Life-Hopes* (Oxford: Oxford University Press, 1988), chapter 9 and passim.

moral law and really ought to mend his ways, but also little reason to believe that mere hortatory reminders to offenders of what they already know *ever* have much effect on their behavior. In Pereboom's world without blame, by contrast, the prospects for successful jawboning are evidently brighter. In that pastel world, friendly persuasion works.

The deepest oddity about Pereboom's world, however, lies not in any of this, but rather in the fact that the only problems wrongdoing appears to present to its inhabitants are future oriented. That, at any rate, is the clear implication of the three responses to wrongdoing—admonish, ignore, walk away—that Pereboom is willing to countenance; for all three recommend themselves primarily as methods of preserving our future tranquility. This exclusively future-oriented stance toward wrongdoing, reminiscent of some of what Strawson says about the objective attitude, is bound to seem profoundly strange to anyone to whom the primary significance of wrongdoing lies not in what it augurs but simply in what it is. To such a person—that is, to all of us in our philosophically unguarded moments—nothing less than actual blame will do.

The fact that we find it disorienting to imagine a world without blame is neither a vindication of our current outlook nor a refutation of Pereboom's recommendations for change; but it does confirm the impression that blame is somehow central to our actual moral lives. Further confirmation, if any is needed, can be found in the extraordinary lengths to which we are willing to go to affix and avoid blame. Many a negotiation, on issues ranging from divorce settlements to the fate of international refugees, has broken down precisely over who is to blame. Reflecting on these facts, we are naturally led to wonder *why* blame is as central to our lives as it evidently is.

That is the question I ultimately want to answer. However, before I can get to it, I will have to explore a number of other, more specific questions. These include not only the surprisingly unexplored question of what blame itself is, but important ancillary questions about persons, actions, character, morality, and various other topics. To bring these questions into focus, let us return to the contrast between blame and the surrogates Pereboom proposes. When we blame someone, exactly what do we add to the bare belief that he has acted wrongly?

II

Formally, blame is a stance or attitude that a person takes toward himself or another on the basis of a judgment that that person has in some way failed to conform to some moral standard. I offer this formula not because the phrase "a stance or attitude" conveys any real information—it is obviously just a placeholder—but rather because the formula's logical complexity highlights what is present in blame but absent from its Pereboom-approved surrogates. One way to put the difference is to say that whereas the Pereboom surrogates are all reactions *to the wrongness of what a person has done*, blame has the essentially more complicated structure of being a reaction *to a person on the basis of the wrongness of what he has done*. Another, more familiar way of putting the point is that the Pereboom-surrogates are all directed at the sin while genuine blame is directed at the sinner.

This structural contrast immediately clarifies what is at issue; for it allows us to see exactly why abandoning blame would mean thinking of wrongdoing in a radically new way. The novelty, we can see, would lie in our rejection of the assumption that the moral significance of a wrong act is bound up with its relation to the agent. This is the assumption upon which we rely when we take the wrongness of what a person does to justify us in condemning him. However, we would no longer be making that assumption if we came to react to bad behavior exclusively by condemning *it*; for in that case our condemnation would never reach as far as the agent himself. To abandon blame while continuing to deplore wrong acts would evidently be to substitute some view to the effect that such acts are freestanding evils for our current assumption that they reflect badly on the agents who perform them.[5]

Given the centrality of this assumption, one obvious question about blame is whether any wrong act *is* related to an agent in a way

---

5. Compare Bernard Williams: "Blame needs an occasion—an action—and a target—the person who did the action and who goes on from the action to meet the blame. That is its nature; as one might say, its conceptual form." In Bernard Williams, "Nietzsche's Minimalist Moral Psychology," in his *Making Sense of Humanity and Other Philosophical Papers* (Cambridge: Cambridge University Press, 1995), 72.

that justifies the transfer of our opprobrium from it to him. Because acts and agents differ in such fundamental ways—because an act is short-lived and displays a relatively simple purposive structure, while an agent is temporally enduring and has a psychology with a vastly more complicated structure—it is not at all obvious why the moral defects of a mere act should cast a negative shadow on anything as substantial as an agent. A *fortiori*, it is not obvious why the moral defects of a past act, which no longer exists, should cast a negative shadow on an agent who still does exist. If this relation cannot be clarified—if we cannot bridge the gap between sin and sinner—then Pereboom's view that we should condemn only wrong acts but not the agents who perform them may win by default.[6]

Moreover, even if the relation can be clarified, a number of further questions will remain. It is one thing to elucidate the assumption on which blame rests and quite another to explain what blame itself is. The question of what we are doing when we blame someone, which I deferred by introducing the placeholder description "a stance or attitude," is much harder than it looks. As I have already intimated, we cannot answer this question by calling attention to the way blame feels because we sometimes blame people without feeling anything, and we cannot answer it by calling attention to the purpose of blaming because blame typically serves *no* purpose. What the other possibilities are, and whether any of them might yield a more satisfactory account, is not immediately clear.

The questions raised so far—"what is the relation between an agent and his act that we take to justify us in blaming him for it?" and "what are we doing when we blame him?"—are partly analytical, partly factual, and partly normative. By contrast, the main reason for asking these questions is straightforwardly normative. The point of

---

6. Pereboom's own view is that the current assumption is untenable because it is incompatible with determinism. His reason for denying that any act can reflect badly on an agent in a way that makes blame appropriate is that "since determinism is true, we lack the freedom required for moral responsibility" ("Determinism *al Dente*," 243–44). I think Pereboom is wrong about this, but do not intend to argue the point. My aim, as I have said, is to bypass the perennial question of whether the truth of determinism would compel us to reject the assumption that an act's badness can reflect badly on the agent in favor of the fresher and less-discussed question of whether we have any positive reason to accept that assumption.

trying to understand blame is not just that blaming is among the things people find it hard not to do—so too, after all, are laughing, digesting, and being bored—but is rather that wrongdoers are often thought to *deserve* blame. What really interests us is not blame but blameworthiness, and this notion poses yet another difficult set of questions. Fully to understand blameworthiness, we will have to ask both why blame is so often viewed as an appropriate response to wrongdoing and whether such beliefs are ever really justified.

I will turn shortly to what I intend to say about each question. However, before I do, I want to make two preliminary points, one terminological and the other methodological. The terminological point concerns my description of the sorts of acts that render agents blameworthy. Up to now, I have referred to those acts simply as wrong. However, this description is inaccurate, since a person may deserve no blame for performing a wrong act for which he has an excuse. When someone does something wrong, what determines whether he is blameworthy is (roughly) whether he was capable of recognizing and responding to the reasons for not doing it.[7] To mark this complication, I will refer to the morally defective acts that render agents blameworthy not as *wrong* acts but rather as *bad* ones. However, because the corresponding phrase "bad actor" is ambiguous between "bad person who acts" and "person who acts badly," I will refer to those who perform bad acts not as bad actors but rather as wrongdoers.

The other preliminary point—the methodological one—concerns a problem that my guiding questions collectively raise. Put most simply, the problem is that we seem unable to answer any one of these questions without presupposing answers to the others. It would, for example, be hard to clarify the relation between an agent and a bad act that makes it reasonable to blame him for it unless we already had some idea of why it

---

7. Although I don't think that having acted wrongly is either necessary or sufficient for blameworthiness, I do think that any adequate statement of the necessary or sufficient conditions for being blameworthy will have to make essential reference to acts that are wrong. At least to this extent, I take the concept of wrongness to be prior to that of blameworthiness. For an account which defines wrongness in terms of blameworthiness, and thus reverses this ordering, see Allan Gibbard, *Wise Feelings, Apt Choices* (Cambridge, Mass.: Harvard University Press, 1990), 40–45.

is reasonable to blame him; and this in turn requires a prior understanding of what blame itself is. Conversely, we will not be able to say much about what blame is unless we already have a grip on the act/agent relation that it presupposes and the notion of blameworthiness in which it is embedded; and neither again can we say much about blameworthiness unless we know a good deal about both what blame is and the relation between wrongdoers and their bad acts that is supposed to render them worthy of it. Because our questions are so closely interrelated, it is not obvious where our discussion of them should begin.

One way to avoid having to break into the circle would be to propose an integrated view that simultaneously provides answers to all of the questions. By taking this holistic approach, we may seem able to avoid reliance on either unclarified terms or undefended assumptions. It seems to me, however, that the holistic approach would gain us no real ground; for the same problems would only reappear as soon as we tried to defend our integrated set of answers. In any event, I will not attempt to sidestep the difficulty by simultaneously proposing answers to all of the questions.

Instead, my approach will be to proceed in stages. In the first stage, I will defer any attempt to offer either a substantive theory of the nature of blame or a reconstruction of the normative underpinnings of blameworthiness. Instead of theorizing about either notion, I will rely on our intuitive understanding of each. This will enable me to concentrate on clarifying the relation between agents and their bad acts that must obtain if the unanalyzed notions are to apply. Then, in the second stage, I will take up the remaining questions. Although I will begin by asking what blame is, my answers will be integrated in that I will require of any acceptable account of blame that it explain why blame is something of which wrongdoers are thought worthy. By taking this stepwise approach, I will attempt to arrive at an account that explains exactly what we would lose if we were to make the transition to a world without blame.

III

As I have said, the first stage of my discussion — chapters 2 through 4 — will deal with the question of how the badness of a mere act can ever justify the condemnation that we direct at the agent. Let me now be more specific about how the argument at this stage will run.

Although the relation between agents and their bad acts poses problems for libertarians and compatibilists alike, only some compatibilists have taken the problems seriously. There is a well-known strand of compatibilist thought, represented most prominently by David Hume, according to which the reason we are often justified in blaming wrongdoers is that the badness of their acts is often traceable to corresponding defects in their characters.[8] For example, when someone acts cruelly or dishonestly, the reason we are justified in blaming him is that his behavior reveals that *he himself* is to a degree cruel or dishonest. Although this proposal is usually advanced to explain why we can blame agents for their *past* bad acts—the proffered explanation is that whatever bad traits a wrongdoer has manifested in the past are likely to persist—it obviously also applies to the logically prior question of why it is reasonable to condemn agents for whatever bad acts they perform right now. Thus, by accepting the current proposal, we can give a single answer to both the synchronic and the diachronic versions of our question.

Given its specificity and comprehensiveness, Hume's proposal is the obvious place to begin. Unfortunately, despite its advantages, the proposal as presented is vulnerable to two crippling objections. One important reason to reject it is that the magnitude of the character flaw that a person's bad act manifests bears no necessary relation to, and so can hardly be said to explain, the degree to which he is *blameworthy* for performing the act. A trivial flaw can give rise to a seriously blameworthy act and vice versa. A further and no less serious objection is that if what rendered a wrongdoer blameworthy were simply the persisting character flaw that he manifests by acting badly, then each wrongdoer would be no less blameworthy than he actually is if he had the same flaw but had had no opportunity to manifest it in action. This implication is damning because it shows Hume to be committed to the view that what really justifies us in blaming a wrongdoer has nothing to do with what he actually does.

8. See David Hume, *A Treatise of Human Nature*, ed. L. A. Selby-Bigge (Oxford: Oxford University Press, 1960), book II, part III, sec. II; and David Hume, *An Inquiry Concerning Human Understanding*, ed. Charles W. Hendel (Indianapolis, Ind.: Bobbs-Merrill, 1955), sec. VIII, part II.

Both objections to Hume's proposal will be developed at some length in chapter 2. However, my main aim in raising them is not to show where the proposal goes wrong, but is rather to highlight two invaluable insights that I take it to contain. Of these two insights, the first is that a person's character, which is at once an enduring aspect of him and a dynamic contributor to each of his actions, is uniquely well situated to mediate between him and his bad acts. The second is that a person's bad behavior need not exhaust the things for which he can be blamed. These insights will form the bases, respectively, of the constructive arguments of chapters 3 and 4.

The central challenge for anyone who takes a wrongdoer's character to be what mediates between him and his bad act is to show how the act's badness can be neither so direct a consequence of his bad character as to warrant no independent condemnation nor so distinct from his character as to warrant only condemnation that does not extend to him. To meet the first half of this challenge, I will emphasize the ways in which a bad act can result from the interplay of various aspects of the agent's character, none which is itself bad; to meet the second, I will argue that when the elements of someone's character do so interact, the badness of what he does is traceable to him in just the way that blame's justification appears to require. By assigning character this reduced but still substantial role, we will take a major step toward preserving what is true and important about Hume's proposal while avoiding its defects.

And we will take an additional step by embracing the further thesis that agents can be blamed for their bad traits *as well as* their bad acts. Although this thesis has the virtue of analytical clarity—it cleanly separates two claims that the original Humean proposal runs together—many would reject it on the grounds that we cannot reasonably blame people for bad traits they cannot help having. To block this objection, some insist that even those whose vices are now intractable were once able to prevent them from developing. It seems to me, however, that this response is based largely on wishful thinking—that in actuality we rarely exercise effective control over the development of our traits. For this reason, I will argue in chapter 4 that the more promising response is to reject the premise that people only deserve blame for what they can or once could control. In offering this rejoinder, I do not mean to suggest that people ever deserve blame for *acts* over which they never exercised control, but I do mean that the reason we cannot blame them for such acts turns on considerations that are peculiar to action. Because the control requirement applies only in the context of agency, it does not govern the justification of blame in general.

IV

By invoking character to bridge the act/agent gap, we can explain how the badness of what a person does may reflect negatively on him. This justifies the assumption that distinguishes blame from the reactions that Pereboom wants to substitute for it. However, it does not explain either what blame is or (therefore) why a wrongdoer or bad person might be thought worthy of it. These are the questions to which I will turn in the second half of the book.

Unlike the relation between bad acts and blameworthy agents, the question of what blame is has elicited a number of philosophical responses, and in chapter 5 I will survey the most important of these. One familiar proposal, favored by some utilitarians, is that what we are doing when we blame someone is expressing our disapproval of his behavior or character in a way that we hope will change it. Another, very different view is that what blaming someone adds to believing that he has acted badly or is a bad person is some sort of further belief—for example, that his misbehavior has somehow stained his "moral record" or reduced his "moral balance." Yet a third proposal is that blame is essentially an affective phenomenon—that to blame a wrongdoer is to react to him by "withdrawing one's good will" (Strawson's phrase) or with anger, hostility, or some other negative emotion. Although each proposal can be developed in various ways, each is vulnerable to objections that extend to all its variants. The defects in each case seem deep and irremediable.

Like my discussion of Hume's proposal in chapter 2, the discussion in chapter 5 will be mainly critical. However, also like the discussion in chapter 2, this discussion is meant not to be destructive but to point the way to something better. Thus, the obvious next question is what the deficiencies of the familiar ways of thinking about blame can teach us. That is the question I will try to answer in chapter 6.

Because we can blame a wrongdoer without either feeling or expressing any anger toward him, we cannot take either anger or its expression to be what blaming someone adds to believing that he has acted badly. For similar reasons, we cannot locate the missing element in such common reactions as reproaching the wrongdoer or (in cases of self-blame) apologizing for his action. However, even if none of these reactions are essential to blame, each is often associated with it, and that itself may be an important clue. Given that anger, hostile gestures, reprimands, and the rest are so often associated with blame, we may reasonably suppose that anyone who blames someone must at least be *disposed* to react to him in each of these ways. This raises the possibility that what blaming someone adds to believing that he has acted badly or is a bad person may simply be the presence of the corresponding dispositions.

By taking anger, reproach, and the rest to be related to blame only as reactions that blamers are disposed to have, we arrive at an account that assigns each an important role without implying that any is essential to blame. As I shall argue in chapter 6, this is a major step forward. However, as I shall also argue, we cannot leave things here because if we did, we would not be able to explain why these dispositions cluster together, why such clusters rate a concept of their own, or why the instancing of that concept is morally important. To explain all this, and thus to realize the promise of the dispositional approach, we must somehow augment that approach by tracing each blame-related disposition to a single source.

And that is just what I will try to do. Put baldly and without argument, the view that I will defend is that each such disposition is explicable in light of a single type of desire-belief pair—a pair whose components are, first, the familiar belief that the person in question has acted badly or has a bad character, but also, second, a corresponding desire that that person *not* have acted badly or *not* have a bad character. If the crucial organizing role of the latter desires has not been noticed, the reason is probably that they are oriented to the past or present, both of which are fixed and unchangeable, and so do not seem capable of motivating us. However, as I shall argue in some detail, this last inference is much too quick. When the desires are combined with the appropriate beliefs, they are capable of giving rise to just the dispositions by which blame is standardly marked.

This two-tiered account of blame, which takes it to consist of a characteristic set of affective and behavioral dispositions that are organized around an equally characteristic type of desire-belief pair, resolves many unanswered questions. It explains why blame has no essential phenomenology yet remains closely linked to anger and resentment, why it can be kept entirely private yet is useful as a form of social control, why it always involves, yet is never exhausted by, a belief about a person's bad behavior or character, and so on. However, the most important question about blame—is it really something of which a wrongdoer or bad person can be worthy?—remains to be addressed. In the book's seventh and concluding chapter, I will test my account of blame against this final question. Although I will not try to show that anyone actually is blameworthy—to do that, I would have to defuse the threat of determinism—I will at least try to explain what it would be for someone to be blameworthy if blame itself is what I think it is.

To bring this out, my strategy will be to work backwards from what I think blame itself is to an account of why someone might be worthy of it. Because I take the core of each instance of blame to consist of a certain belief and a certain corresponding desire, the central question here is how a bad act or trait can call for each member of this pair. Where the pair's belief-component is concerned, the relevant norm is that of accuracy: a belief that someone has acted badly or is a bad person is appropriate when and because the belief would be true if it were held. Where the pair's desire-component is concerned, the key fact is that morality is a system that claims authority over all persons at all times and whose reasons purport to override all others. Because morality has these hegemonic aspirations, we cannot fully accept a moral principle without wanting those whom we take to have ignored or flouted it not to have done so and those whom we take to be disposed to ignore or flout it not to be so disposed. Thus, if we are *justified* in accepting a moral principle, then we must also be justified in having a blame-constituting desire whenever we correctly believe that it *has* been flouted, ignored, and so on.

Taken together, these considerations suggest a satisfying account of blameworthiness. Very roughly, what the account says is that to be blameworthy is to have done something, or to have some trait, that both (a) makes true a certain blame-constituting belief and (b) violates the moral principle whose justification supports the corresponding blame-constituting desire. By accepting this account, we will do justice to our intuitions about specific cases, bring together the reasons for acting morally and for blaming those who do not, and explain why there continues to be disagreement about whether determinism precludes blameworthiness. Of course, precisely because the account does not resolve the free will question, it does not establish that anyone actually is blameworthy. However, what it does show is that the only conditions under which blame would not be appropriate would also be conditions in which morality itself could gain no purchase. If morality has a claim on us, then blame is also in place; if we must view morality as having a claim, then we must resist the blandishments of a world without blame.

TWO

■ ■ ■

WHEN GOOD PEOPLE DO
BAD THINGS

Actions are by their very nature temporary and perishing; and where they proceed not from some cause in the characters and disposition of the person, who perform'd them, they infix not themselves upon him, and can neither redound to his honour, if good, nor infamy, if evil. The action itself may be blameable; it may be contrary to all the rules of morality and religion: But the person is not responsible for it; and as it proceeded from nothing in him, that is durable or constant, and leaves nothing of that nature behind it, 'tis impossible he can, upon its account, become the object of punishment or vengeance.[1]

IN THIS PASSAGE, HUME EXPRESSED THE VAGUE BUT COMPELLING THOUGHT that however badly someone acts, we cannot blame him unless the bad act somehow "proceeded from" his character. Although the writing in the passage is characteristically loose, we may reasonably take Hume to have meant, first, that no act can render an agent blameworthy unless it originated in some *vice or defect* in the agent's character—Hume added a bit later that "actions render a person criminal, merely as they are proofs of criminal passions or principles in the mind"[2]—and, second, that the respect in which the agent's character is defective must match the respect in which his act is bad. As so interpreted, Hume was saying that we cannot blame someone for lying unless he is in some measure dishonest; for behaving in a cowardly manner unless he is to some

---

1. David Hume, *A Treatise of Human Nature*, ed. L. A. Selby-Bigge (Oxford: Oxford University Press, 1960), book II, part III, sec. II, 411. An almost identical passage can be found in Hume, *An Inquiry Concerning Human Understanding*, ed. Charles W. Hendel (Indianapolis, Ind.: Bobbs-Merrill, 1955), sec. VIII, part II, 107.

2. Ibid., 412.

degree a coward; or for acting cruelly unless he has a cruel streak. This view—henceforth BC—has also been endorsed by R. E. Hobart, Richard Brandt, and Robert Nozick, among others.[3]

Given the problem Hume was trying to solve, it is not hard to see why he might be drawn to BC. As his reference to the "temporary and perishing" nature of action makes clear, the question that interested him was how it can be reasonable to condemn a temporally enduring person for what is merely a transient bad act.[4] Why, if someone is no longer acting badly, does it remain reasonable to condemn him for what he previously did? To answer this question, Hume had to invoke some suitably tight connection between what is enduring about the agent and what was bad about his previous act; and by insisting that the act be one that manifested a flaw in the agent's character, he put himself in a position to do just that. Because a person's character is largely stable over time, any character flaw that he manifested by acting badly in the past is likely to provide both a natural link between him then and him now and a natural basis upon which to condemn him now.[5]

But this is not the only reason to find BC attractive. As I remarked in the previous chapter, BC also seems relevant to the simpler but more fundamental question of why we are justified in condemning the

---

3. See R. E. Hobart, "Will as Involving Determination and Inconceivable Without It," in *Free Will and Determinism*, ed. Bernard Berofsky (New York: Harper and Row, 1966), 63–95; Richard Brandt, "Blameworthiness and Obligation," in *Essays in Moral Philosophy*, ed. A. I. Melden (Seattle: University of Washington Press, 1958), 3–39; and Robert Nozick, *Philosophical Explanations* (Cambridge, Mass.: Harvard University Press, 1981), 383 ff.

4. That this was Hume's question is evident from the quotation with which I began. That it was Hobart's is evident from such passages as these: "Morality has its eye upon acts, but an act is fleeting, it cannot be treasured and cherished. A quality can be, it lasts" ("Free Will as Involving Determination," 84); "If in conceiving the self you detach it from all motives or tendencies, what you have is not a morally admirable or condemnable, not a morally characterisable self at all. Hence it is not subject to reproach" (ibid., 68–69).

5. In addition, as others have noted, Hume's proposal has the further advantage of providing a natural explanation of why many familiar excuses render blame *inappropriate*; for the force of many excuses is precisely to imply that the agent did *not* manifest the relevant character flaw. See in this connection Brandt, "Blameworthiness and Obligation" and Nozick, *Philosophical Explanations*.

wrongdoer—as opposed to his wrongdoing—*at all*. By accepting BC, we put ourselves in a position to say that when an agent acts badly, what justifies us in condemning him is precisely the vice or bad trait that his bad act manifests. I think, in fact, that Hume himself was committed to just this view, since if our rationale for condemning someone who acted badly in the past is that he still has the character flaw that his past bad act manifested, then our rationale for condemning someone *when* he acts badly must similarly be that he *then* has the corresponding character flaw. However, the important question about the view is, of course, not whether Hume or anyone else was committed to it, but rather whether it is defensible.

II

Is the view defensible? Should we agree that what justifies us in condemning a wrongdoer, as opposed to his bad behavior, is precisely the character defect that the bad behavior manifests? As I have already intimated, I think we must reject this view. However, before I can give my reasons, I must resolve two unclarities in my formulation of BC.

The first unclarity concerns BC's logical form. As expressed, BC is conditional in only one direction. It says that someone is blameworthy only if his bad act manifests a corresponding character flaw, but not that someone is blameworthy if, or whenever, his bad act manifests a character flaw. However, if BC is to explain why agents who act badly are blameworthy—if we are to say that what justifies us in condemning a person who acts badly *just is* the character flaw that his bad act manifests—then the existence of such a flaw must be sufficient as well as necessary to justify our condemnation. Thus, to serve the current purpose, BC must be biconditional: it must say that when someone acts badly, he is blameworthy *if and only if* his bad act manifests a corresponding character flaw.

The second (and messier) of the two unclarities concerns the *meaning* of "character flaw." How, exactly, should we understand this term? There are actually two issues here, in that any adequate answer will have to include both an interpretation of "character" and an account of what it means to call a character flawed. I shall briefly consider each issue in turn.

"Character" has no canonical meaning. Given the recent revival of interest in virtue ethics, there may be some temptation to think of it exclusively in terms of virtue and vice. However, despite its usefulness for some purposes, this narrow interpretation of "character" is neither unavoidable nor standard. As Joel Kupperman has pointed out,

> It would be a mistake to link the concept of character too closely to morality.... A tendency to rebound or not to rebound from failure, for example, is not normally judged as morally virtuous or the reverse. Yet something of this sort can play a major role in our account of character.[6]

Although ordinary usage does not speak with a single voice, Kupperman is surely right to suggest that character is often taken to include not only moral virtues and vices, but also many morally neutral tendencies. Indeed, on one familiar view, a person's character encompasses his whole characteristic set of cognitive, affective, and behavioral dispositions—the whole collection of interrelated tendencies that together make him the person he is.

This maximally broad interpretation may also not be fully faithful to common usage. It may, for example, classify as elements of character some dispositions that are more usually taken to fall under personality. However, for our purposes, what matters about an interpretation of "character" is not its fidelity to common speech, but rather its consistency with the most plausible version(s) of the proposed explanation of why we are justified in condemning wrongdoers. Because the maximally broad interpretation will allow us the widest possible latitude both in the interpretation of BC and in the formulation of alternative proposals, I will adopt that interpretation in the discussion that follows.

Bearing this interpretation in mind, and reserving for the next chapter any discussion of alternatives, let us turn next to the question of what it is to have a bad or a defective character. As has often been pointed out, a person can have a bad character without having a history of acting badly. Someone who has never displayed cowardice may simply never have had to face danger, while "[a] person may be greedy, envious, cowardly, cold, ungenerous, unkind, vain, or conceited, but *behave* perfectly by a monumental effort of will."[7] Hence, any remotely

---

6. Joel Kupperman, *Character* (New York: Oxford University Press, 1991), 7–8.
7. Thomas Nagel, "Moral Luck," in his *Mortal Questions* (Cambridge: Cambridge University Press, 1979), 32.

adequate account of what it is to have a character defect must focus not merely on what a person has done but also on what he would do in various circumstances—on his dispositions to behave rather than his behavior itself—while any more than remotely adequate account must further widen its scope to encompass the person's dispositions not only to behave but also to notice and feel. To be a cruel person, on a view that takes all this into account, is (at the least) to be disposed to notice vulnerability in others, to exploit it by causing them to suffer, and to take pleasure in their suffering, all in a broad and diverse range of conditions.

Because having a defective character involves having a number of distinct dispositions, each of which can obtain in a wider or narrower range of conditions, there is more than one continuum along which each form of badness can vary. Thus, in theory, there are indefinitely many possible interpretations of BC. To bring some order to this unruly situation, I will concentrate exclusively on the dispositions most directly relevant to our topic—dispositions actually to perform the relevant sorts of bad acts—and will, in addition, restrict my attention to the near-maximal, near-median, and near-minimal forms of these dispositions. Expressed informally, what the corresponding versions of BC assert is that an agent is blameworthy if and only if his bad act (a) manifests a vice; (b) manifests a bad tendency; and (c) shows that he "has it in him" to perform a bad act of the relevant sort. Put a bit more formally, what they come to is:

BC1: Someone who acts badly is blameworthy if and only if his bad act manifests a disposition to perform bad acts of the relevant sort in a broad enough range of conditions to qualify him as having the corresponding vice.

BC2: Someone who acts badly is blameworthy if and only if his bad act manifests a disposition to perform bad acts of the relevant sort in some significant range of conditions.

BC3: Someone who acts badly is blameworthy if and only if his bad act manifests a disposition to perform bad acts of the relevant sort in exactly the conditions that prevail when he acts.

If none of these versions of BC is capable of sustaining the proposed explanation of why we are justified in condemning agents when they act badly, then no other version is likely to be capable of doing so either.

Moreover, in fact, none of the three versions is capable of sustaining the proposed explanation; for each is either too narrow or too broad to capture our intuitions about which agents are blameworthy. If we opt for BC1 or BC2, then we will have to accept the counterintuitive implication that we cannot blame good people when they do bad things; while if we opt for BC3, then we will be saddled with the equally counterintuitive implication that we can blame even good people who do *not* do bad things. To show that BC1, BC2, and BC3 have these implications, and thus to bring out the problems with the proposed explanation, I shall now examine each version of BC in more detail.

III

BC1, which says that an agent is not blameworthy unless his bad act manifests the corresponding vice, need not detain us long. As many have noted, even virtuous people sometimes perform bad acts that are "out of character,"[8] and when they do, their virtue does not exempt them from blame. We might, for example, be warranted in blaming an honest person who at one point told a self-serving lie, a brave soldier who on one occasion deserted his post, or a kind person who once said something cruel. The blameworthiness of these agents poses problems for BC1 because having a virtue such as honesty, courage, or kindness is flatly incompatible with having the opposing vice. If someone is disposed to tell the truth under a broad enough range of circumstances to qualify as honest, he cannot also be disposed to lie under a broad enough range of circumstances to qualify as *dis*honest; and the same is true, *mutatis mutandis*, of someone who is brave or kind. Because a virtuous person who acts "out of character" is thus incapable of satisfying BC1's requirement that he manifest the corresponding vice, BC1

---

8. For example, in a discussion critical of virtue ethics, Robert B. Louden has written that "[b]ecause the emphasis in agent ethics is on long-term, characteristic patterns of behavior, its advocates run the risk of overlooking occasional lies or acts of selfishness on the grounds that such performances are mere temporary aberrations—acts out of character." In Robert B. Louden, "On Some Vices of Virtue Ethics," in *Virtue Ethics*, ed. Roger Crisp and Michael Slote (Oxford: Oxford University Press, 1997), 209.

implies, implausibly, that we are never warranted in blaming an honest person who uncharacteristically lies, a brave soldier who uncharacteristically flees from danger, or a kind person who uncharacteristically lashes out cruelly.

By contrast, BC2, which says only that an agent is not blameworthy unless his bad act manifests a disposition to perform similar acts under some significant range of conditions, does *not* imply that we can never blame a virtuous person when he acts "out of character"; for it is not at all inconsistent to say, on the one hand, that a given agent is disposed to act honestly, bravely, or kindly in a broad enough range of conditions to qualify as honest, brave, or kind, but that, on the other hand, there is some limited but significant range of conditions in which he is disposed to act very differently. Someone may, for example, be honest about everything except conveying bad news, brave about everything except public speaking, and kind to everyone except his ex-wife. If such a person has not previously had to deliver bad news, address an audience, or deal with his ex-wife, then the dishonesty, cowardice, and cruelty that he displays in these situations may seem shockingly uncharacteristic. Nevertheless, each act may, for all that, still manifest a disposition to perform similar acts in a significant enough range of conditions to satisfy BC2. Thus, BC2, unlike BC1, can indeed accommodate some of the cases in which good people do bad things.

It cannot, however, accommodate them all; for although many of the relevant agents are disposed to perform similar acts in significant ranges of other conditions, many others are not. In cases of the latter sort, the agent's uncharacteristic bad act is traceable not to a bad streak in his character, but rather to the interaction of certain highly specific situational factors with various fine-grained dispositions, *none* of which is a disposition to perform bad acts of the relevant sort. To grasp the familiar reality that this rather abstract formula expresses, consider the following three cases, in each of which a kind person acts cruelly on a single occasion.

> *Case 1.* Alphonse is a generous and empathetic person, but is also a tormented soul. He is someone who feels compromised by even unintended lapses from moral perfection, who judges himself extremely harshly, and who tends to express his harsh judgments in self-destructive ways. Knowing that he is prone to downward spirals, Alphonse tries scrupulously to do the right thing. However, on one

occasion, he unwittingly acquires a piece of information he should not have and, though in fact blameless, predictably begins to feel worthless and anomic. Acting in a spirit of moral self-defilement, Alphonse makes a cruel remark of precisely the kind that he most abhors.

Case 2. Barbaroo, too, is generous and empathetic, but there the resemblance to Alphonse ends. Far from being tormented, Barbaroo is if anything a bit smug. Secure in his own rectitude, he occasionally erupts with righteous indignation; but when he does, he fights fairly and does not exploit his keen ability to discern where others are vulnerable. Even when an opponent is cruel, Barbaroo normally has no impulse to retaliate. Still, even Barbaroo has his limits, and one day they are reached. A colleague has been grossly irresponsible and, confronted, has reacted with hurtful insults. Job pressures and fatigue make emotional short cuts attractive. Hard pressed, Barbaroo acts on what is for him a rare impulse of retaliatory cruelty.

Case 3. Celeste, the youngest of our trio, is a person of ready and generous sympathy. However, Celeste is also given to enthusiasms, the most recent of which is a misguided confidence in the transformative power of searing honesty. Thus, confronted with someone who is both unattractive and self-conscious about it, Celeste does not accede to her strong inclination to steer the conversation to a safer topic, but plunges resolutely into a disquisition on the need to face up to the misfortune of ugliness. Although her native kindness re-asserts itself in mid-disquisition, her interlocutor has by then caught her drift, and things have gotten tense. Because Celeste reacts to tension by losing her verbal suppleness, she cannot quite find the words to avert disaster when she realizes, too late, what she is doing.

Although each case has been described in some detail, all three remain sketchy and underdeveloped. A closer examination would re-veal the myriad of still finer-grained dispositions that shape each agent's interpretation of his situation, and his reactions to it, at each unfolding stage. Nevertheless, despite their sketchiness, the three cases are different enough to make it clear that there are many ways in which a bad act of any given type can be the result of the successive activation of various dispositions, none of which is a disposition to perform similar acts under any significant range of conditions. For example, the dispositions that come together to produce Alphonse's cruel remark—his dispositions to hold himself to unrealistic moral standards, judge himself harshly when he falls short, and react to self-condemnation with self-immolation—are not themselves dispositions to act cruelly; and neither (we may suppose) would their interaction lead Alphonse to act cruelly under many other circumstances. *Mutatis mutandis*, the same may hold for Barbaroo and Celeste. If it does, and if we define "character" broadly enough to encompass all of the relevant dispositions, then we can truly say of each agent both that cruelty is no part *of* his character and that this particular cruel act is firmly rooted *in* his character.

IV

Because Alphonse, Barbaroo, and Celeste are not disposed to act cruelly in any significant ranges of conditions—because none of their characters contain even a streak of cruelty—neither BC1 nor BC2 can account for the intuition that they are blameworthy. However, because the cruel act that each performs can be traced to the interaction of a number of his fine-grained dispositions with various aspects of his situation, each of them is manifesting a disposition to act cruelly in conditions exactly like the ones that prevail when he acts. Not coincidentally, this is precisely the sort of disposition that BC3 takes to render an agent blameworthy. Thus, of our three versions of BC, only BC3 interprets character flaws narrowly enough to allow us to condemn even a virtuous agent whose bad act is maximally "out of character."

Does this mean that BC3 succeeds where its predecessors fail? Before I can answer this question, I must forestall a possible misunderstanding. As I have expressed it, BC3 asserts that someone who acts badly is blameworthy if and only if his bad act manifests a disposition to perform bad acts of just that sort in conditions just like the ones that then prevail. However, the fact that it is just these conditions in which the agent is disposed to act badly is clearly irrelevant; he obviously would be no less blameworthy if he were disposed to perform the same sort of act in some other set of conditions. Thus, properly understood, what BC3 takes to render an agent blameworthy is not his being disposed to act badly in *these particular* conditions, but only his being disposed to do so in *one or another* set of conditions.

However, if so, then just as BC1 and BC2 allowed us to blame too few people, BC3 will allow us to blame far too many. To bring this out—to show, indeed, that BC3 is far *more* overinclusive than BC1 and BC2 are underinclusive—we need only remind ourselves of how often BC3's sufficient condition for blameworthiness is satisfied.

Although I cannot prove it, I suspect that for (just about) every person and (just about) every type of bad act, there is some conceivable set of conditions under which that person would perform an act of that type. If this conjecture is correct, then BC3 will imply that virtually all of us are just as blameworthy as any moral monster. Moreover, even if the conjecture is overly pessimistic—even if many people would under no circumstances blind the witnesses to their crimes, bludgeon their children to death, or participate in "ethnic cleansing"—something like it pretty clearly holds for many less spectacular evils. That this is so is suggested both by empirical studies such as the Milgram experiments, which showed that under the right circumstances most people can be brought to do things that they (and we) consider wrong,[9] and by the commonsense observation that we are, most of us, at least no better than Alphonse, Barbaroo, and Celeste. Thus, even under the most conservative of assumptions, accepting BC3 would mean drastically expanding the range of persons whom we take to be blameworthy. Because BC3 grounds our condemnation of the wrongdoer in his possession of a type of disposition that most of the rest of us also have, it has the counterintuitive implication that many whose character and behavior seem unimpeachable are every bit as blameworthy as those who behave very badly.

Not everyone will find this implication disturbing. If someone believes both that it is unfair to blame a person for anything beyond his control and that a person's circumstances are relevantly beyond his control, then he may hold, with Nicholas Rescher, that:

> [t]he person who is prevented by lack of opportunity and occasion alone from displaying cupidity and greed still remains at heart an avaricious person and (as such) merits the condemnation of those

9. The Milgram experiments are discussed in Stanley Milgram, *Obedience to Authority* (New York: Harper and Row, 1974). For useful discussion of Milgram's results and a wide range of relevant others, see John Doris, *Lack of Character* (Cambridge: Cambridge University Press, 2002).

right-thinking people who are in a position actually to know this to be so—if such there are.[10]

To those who reject the possibility of what Thomas Nagel has called "circumstantial moral luck,"[11] BC3's implication that many who do not act badly are just as blameworthy as many who do will actually be welcome.

For the record, I am skeptical about the principle that it is never fair to blame people for what they cannot help. (Some of my reasons for doubt will emerge in chapter 4). I also think it may be inconsistent to invoke this principle to show that wrongdoers are blameworthy only for the bad dispositions that are activated by factors beyond their control but not for the resulting bad acts; for a wrongdoer is unlikely to have any more control over his bad dispositions than he does over the bad acts that manifest them. However, in the current context, what matters is not whether blaming people for either their acts or their dispositions is unfair, but only that we standardly *do not* take good people to be blameworthy for whatever bad things they would do in exceptional circumstances. When we view good people as blameworthy, it is only because we think that they have in fact acted badly. Because our judgments of blameworthiness are restricted in this way, our actual notion of blameworthiness—the one whose rationale we are trying to understand—cannot possibly rest on BC3. If someone were to invoke that principle, he would not be explicating the normative underpinnings of blame as we know it, but would instead be introducing some quite different concept.

V

BC1, BC2, and BC3 all fail to capture important intuitions about blame. Where BC1 and BC2 are concerned, the intuition that remains

---

10. Nicholas Rescher, "Moral Luck," in *Moral Luck*, ed. Daniel Statman (Albany: State University of New York Press, 1993), 155.

11. Nagel, "Moral Luck," 34n.

unaccounted for is that we can appropriately blame even a good person when he acts badly; while where BC3 is concerned, it is rather that we *cannot* appropriately blame a good (though imperfect) person if he does *not* act badly. Taken together, the two difficulties suggest that no single version of BC is likely to be consistent with all of our important intuitions.

But we are not yet in a position to dismiss BC; for nothing yet said shows that we cannot make progress by combining its different versions. We will, of course, be unable to combine them if we continue to view blameworthiness as all-or-nothing; for in that case, the necessary condition for blameworthiness that BC1 imposes—that the agent be disposed to perform similar bad acts in a very broad range of conditions—will rule out the sufficiency of the narrower dispositions specified by BC2 and BC3, while the necessity of the intermediately narrow disposition specified by BC2 will similarly rule out the sufficiency of the very narrow disposition specified by BC3. However, in fact, our ordinary notion of blameworthiness is not all-or-nothing but degreed: it is perfectly coherent to say that although two agents are both blameworthy, one is significantly *more* blameworthy than the other. This suggests that we might view the three concentric sorts of disposition not as competing necessary and sufficient conditions for blameworthiness, but rather as complementary necessary and sufficient conditions for different *degrees* of it. Instead of viewing BC1, BC2, and BC3 as mutually exclusive, we might say of someone who performs a cruel act, that he is maximally blameworthy if and only if he manifests a disposition to act cruelly under a very broad range of conditions; that he is somewhat blameworthy if and only if he manifests a disposition to act cruelly under some significant range of conditions; and that he is minimally blameworthy if and only if he manifests a disposition to act cruelly under just the conditions that prevail when he acts.

Because it is agreeably ecumenical, this combined version of BC has considerable appeal. However, despite its appeal, it will only advance the discussion if it can avoid the objections that defeat its simpler predecessors. Thus, the question we must now ask is whether the combined version of BC can simultaneously accommodate both the intuition that even kind people like Alphonse, Barbaroo, and Celeste are blameworthy when they act cruelly in exceptional circumstances and the intuition that people who have similar characters but who happen not to encounter exceptional circumstances, and so do not act cruelly, are not blameworthy.

Because the combined version implies that anyone who has any disposition to act cruelly is to some degree blameworthy, it cannot entirely accommodate the intuition that a kind person who would act cruelly in certain exceptional circumstances, but who does not encounter those circumstances and so does not act cruelly, is blameless. However, because the combined version takes each person's degree of blameworthiness to depend on the range of conditions in which he would act badly, it does imply that a kind person who would only act cruelly in exceptional circumstances that he never in fact encounters is only minimally blameworthy. Because this implication at least comes close to accommodating the relevant intuition, it may be sufficient to defuse the central objection to BC3.

However, even if it does, the combined version is far less successful at disarming the objections to BC1 and BC2; for because it implies that Alphonse, Barbaroo, and Celeste are also only minimally blameworthy, it is hopelessly incapable of capturing the full range of intuitions that we may have about them. Its implication that they are only minimally blameworthy may indeed match our intuitions if their behavior is merely edged with cruelty—if, for instance, Barbaroo responds to his colleague's insults by remarking that the colleague's own last book was less than enthusiastically received—but it definitely will not do so if their behavior is seriously cruel. If any member of the trio were knowingly to treat another in a way that was deeply hurtful—if, for example, the intensity of Alphonse's self-loathing were to lead him to spend his whole three-hour seminar humiliating an unpopular, unhappy student—then the fact that Alphonse would behave that way in very few other circumstances would not prevent him from being very blameworthy indeed. As this case illustrates and many others confirm, the amount of blame that someone deserves when he behaves badly depends not on how typical of him the bad behavior is but simply on how bad it is.

And because of this, the objection that I have advanced against BC1 and BC2—that they fail to capture the intuition that good people can be blameworthy when they do bad things—will also apply, albeit in slightly altered form, to the combined version of BC. When someone like Alphonse, Barbaroo, or Celeste acts badly, the breadth of his disposition to perform similar bad acts is no more relevant to *how* blameworthy he is than to *whether* he is blameworthy. At least where good people are concerned, whether and to what degree they are blameworthy depends exclusively on how badly they have actually behaved.

VI

So far, we have seen that no version of BC, single or combined, does justice to all our important intuitions about when good people are and are not blameworthy. Even by itself, this is probably enough to discredit the proposal that what justifies us in condemning a wrongdoer is precisely the character defect that his bad act displays. However, in fact, the problems with the proposed explanation go far deeper, for it fails not only when BC's conditions for blameworthiness are not met, but also when they are.

To show this, and thus complete my argument against the proposed explanation, I must add one further member to our cast of characters. Our new character, Donato, is thoroughly cruel. He takes real pleasure in the suffering of others, has a BC1-grade disposition to inflict pain, and is both subtle and inventive at doing so. Because Donato's cruelty is a genuine vice, the blame he deserves when he acts cruelly should pose few problems for the proposed explanation. However, in fact, it is precisely in cases of this sort that the inadequacy of that explanation is most transparent.

For suppose Donato, finding himself alone with a small child, now acts in character and cruelly taunts the child. According to the proposed explanation, what justifies us in condemning Donato is precisely the cruelty that the taunting displays. However, because Donato's being cruel does not depend on his taunting the child—because he would be no less cruel if he had never met the child—the proposed explanation implies that we would now have exactly the same grounds for condemning Donato if he had not taunted the child. Although Donato's taunting is of course evidence *that* he is cruel, our actual basis for condemning him remains exclusively the cruelty *for which* it is evidence. Hence, if we accept the proposed explanation, the question that really interests us—namely, "why are we justified in condemning Donato *for this particular act of taunting*?"—will remain unanswered.

In saying this, I do not mean that the extent of Donato's cruelty has *no* bearing on how blameworthy he is. If we can legitimately blame people for having bad characters at all, then the extent of Donato's cruelty will obviously be relevant to how blameworthy he is for that. My point, rather, is simply that Donato's bad character cannot possibly be our *only* basis for condemning him, since if it were, then his actual bad behavior would drop out as irrelevant. Whatever else we say, we can hardly deny that Donato is more blameworthy when (and after) he taunts the child than he was beforehand; and to justify this claim, we must somehow look beyond the badness of his character to the badness of the taunting itself.

Because the proposed explanation provides no way of doing this, it is, in the end, quite hopeless. However, although we have found decisive reason to reject the claim that a wrongdoer's defective character is what justifies us in condemning him for acting badly, we have found no comparable reason to reject the related but weaker claim that a wrongdoer's character plays *some* important role in justifying the condemnation that we direct at him for acting badly; and neither have we found reason to reject the claim that the wrongdoer's character, if sufficiently bad, is a legitimate further basis upon which to condemn him. I believe, in fact, that these claims are indeed defensible. They represent the substantial element of truth in the rejected explanation, and they account for much of its initial appeal. In the next two chapters, I will defend a version of each in turn.

THREE

■ ■ ■

THE STRUCTURE OF
BLAMEWORTHY ACTION

HUME DEFENDED BC, WHICH STATES THAT AGENTS ARE BLAMEWORTHY ONLY for acts that reflect flaws in their characters, by arguing that a bad act that "proceeded from nothing" in an agent's character would give us no reason to blame him. As we saw, Hume's defense of BC is unsound; for Alphonse, Barbaroo, and Celeste all clearly deserve blame for bad acts that do *not* manifest character flaws. However, we also saw that a conclusion that bears some resemblance to BC may well be correct; for in all three cases, the agent's blameworthy act is in some sense *rooted in* his character. Taking my cue from this, I now want to propose a non-Humean account of the role that character plays in rendering wrongdoers blameworthy. Although there is indeed a connection between character and blameworthy action, it is not the connection that Hume had in mind.

I

A crucial test for any account of blameworthiness is whether it explains how wrongdoers can deserves blame for what they did. The point of introducing Donato was precisely to show that Hume's account fails this test. If what rendered Donato blameworthy were simply the cruelty that he manifested while taunting the child, then we would have exactly the same grounds for condemning him if he had the same character but had never met the child. Thus, on Hume's account, the badness of Donato's actual taunting drops out as irrelevant.

To improve on Hume's account, we must show how (at least some of) the blame that Donato deserves is justified by his taunting itself. There is, of course, a sense in which the justification is simply that Donato did the taunting—that he is the agent who has performed the act. However, merely to invoke the act/agent relation is hardly to meet the challenge of those who believe, with Pereboom, that we may reasonably condemn the act but not the agent. To meet that challenge, we must somehow specify what it is about the act/agent relation that makes it reasonable to extend our condemnation from a bad act to the agent who performed it.

As I have said, I want to defend a non-Humean account of the role that character plays in determining blameworthiness. To situate that account, we may helpfully contrast it with one that is even further removed from what Hume believed—an account that takes character to play *no* essential role in determining whether someone is blameworthy. According to this maximally non-Humean account, an agent's character exhausts its role by supplying him with impulses that he can then decide either to acquiesce in or to resist. The decision to acquiesce or to resist, which will determine whether he is blameworthy, is by hypothesis independently generated. If an agent reacts to a bad impulse by resisting it, then he is not blameworthy; while if he reacts by giving in, then he is blameworthy, but what justifies us in condemning him is not the bad impulse itself but rather his decision to surrender to it.

Although the view I have just sketched has recognizably Kantian overtones, the clearest statement of it that I know has been provided by C. A. Campbell, who once wrote that

> [n]o one denies that [character] determines, at least largely, what things we desire, and again how greatly we desire them. . . . It does not in the least follow that it has any influence whatsoever in determining the act of decision itself—the decision as to whether we shall exert effort or take the easy course of following the bent of our desiring nature.[1]

---

1. C. A. Campbell, *In Defense of Free Will* (London: George Allen and Unwin, 1967), 43.

Although Campbell's statement of the view appears in a defense of libertarianism, his strategy of interposing a decision between a character-generated bad impulse and the ensuing bad act can be detached from his more controversial claim that at least some such decisions are uncaused. Moreover, whether or not we follow Campbell in rejecting determinism, we can, by taking up his claim that the basis of our condemnation is the agent's decision to *act on* his bad impulse, reconnect our condemnation of the agent to what he actually does.

Unlike the Humean view, which renders the action itself superfluous, Campbell's proposal does assign the act's badness a central role in determining the agent's blameworthiness. Unfortunately, in so doing, it also reintroduces our original question of how the badness of an act can justify our condemnation of the agent. It reintroduces this question because the decision that it interposes between the agent and his bad act seems no less independent of the agent than is the bad act itself. Because that decision stands apart from all of the agent's traits, dispositions, beliefs, and desires, we remain without an explanation of how its badness can reflect badly on *him*. Thus, the net effect is simply to replace our original question—how can an act's badness justify us in condemning the agent?—with the equally difficult question of how a decision's badness can justify us in condemning the person who makes it.[2]

The full dimensions of our problem are now before us. If, with Hume, we simply take the blame that we direct at a wrongdoer to be grounded in the badness of his character, then we lack an explanation of how our condemnation of him can depend on what he does; while if, with Campbell, we take the blame that we direct at the wrongdoer to be grounded in the badness of a decision that is detached from his character, then we lack an explanation of how our condemnation of what he does can extend to him. To navigate a path between these alternatives, we must draw back from Hume's claim that our basis for

---

2. Because this difficulty recurs, we cannot solve our problem by simply following Campbell in redirecting our attention from bad acts to the decisions in which they originate. But might Campbell's proposal fare better if we did factor in its libertarian component? Might our justification for condemning someone who acts badly be precisely that his decision to do so *does* represent an exercise of his contracausal freedom?

condemning an agent who acts badly is simply the bad character that his act manifests, but we cannot retreat all the way to Campbell's claim that our basis for condemning him is a decision that stands *opposed* to his character. But is there really room for an intermediate account that treats an agent's character as more than just the source of his bad impulse, yet as less than our whole basis for condemning him?

II

I think, in fact, that there is; for the relation between character and action is more complicated than either of these polar views suggests. Its complexity begins to emerge when we notice that it is perfectly consistent to say, with Campbell, that agents often decide whether to resist

---

Whether or not we believe, with the hard determinist, that someone who acts badly cannot be blamed if his decision has itself been caused by previous events—and, for the record, I do not believe this—it is hard to see how the mere fact that an agent's decision has not been caused by previous events can shed any light on why he can be blamed for it. Because the absence of causation would be purely negative, it could hardly sustain a positive account of how the uncaused decision was connected to the agent. This does not mean that libertarians cannot explain why it is appropriate to blame agents when they act badly; but it does mean that if any version of libertarianism is going to help, it will have to be one that takes acting freely to involve more than not being caused to act by previous events.

Many libertarians, of course, do believe that acting freely involves something more. They believe that to qualify as free, an act must not only not be caused by any combination of previous events, but also must be caused by the agent himself. But when we ask what this new form of causation might involve, and in particular how it might justify extending our condemnation from a bad act to the agent who performs it, these libertarians have little to offer. Their attempts to elucidate agent-causation generally consist either of the provision of unhelpful synonyms (the causation is said to be "immanent" rather than "transeunt") or else of bare repetition: "the difference between the man's causing A, on the one hand, and the event A just happening, on the other, lies in the fact that, in the first case but not the second, the event A *was* caused and was caused by the man" (Roderick Chisholm, "Human Freedom and the Self," in *Reason at Work: Introductory Readings in Philosophy*, 3rd ed., ed. Steven M. Cahn, Patricia Kitcher, George Sher, and Peter Markie [Fort Worth, Tex.: Harcourt Brace, 1996], 540, 542). This dearth of analysis may not discredit the idea of agent-causation—it is, after all, just what we should expect if that notion is primitive—but it does mean that introducing agent-causation will not answer, but will again only reraise, the question we are asking.

or surrender to the bad impulses that their bad characters supply, while also saying, in the spirit of Hume, that such a decision does not come out of nowhere, but can itself be traced to the interplay of many elements of the agent's psychology each of which may differ both from any of his bad impulses and from any bad traits that have given rise to these.

The operative elements of an agent's psychology are, of course, bound to include many of his beliefs and desires; but they are also bound to include many fine-grained dispositions that are distinct from both his beliefs and his desires. These fine-grained dispositions, in their turn, are bound to encompass both many tendencies that operate prior to the formation of belief or desire—for example, the agent's tendencies to notice certain things but not others and to impose a certain interpretive grid upon what he notices—and many other tendencies, such as the agent's characteristic ways of processing information and reacting emotionally, that are standardly activated *by* his beliefs and desires. Because the interaction of a person's desires, beliefs, and fine-grained dispositions is crucial in shaping every decision he makes, it is not obviously absurd to suppose that when someone acts badly, it is precisely the contribution that these mediating elements collectively make to the badness of his act that justifies us in condemning him for it.

Not obviously absurd, but not obviously correct either; for merely to introduce the mediating elements is not yet to explain *how* their contribution to the badness of what an agent does can justify us in condemning him. If the need to explain this is not immediately apparent, it may be because we tend to assume that each set of desires, beliefs, and dispositions whose interaction gives rise to a bad act is bound to contain at least one member that is itself bad. However, one of the things that emerged from our discussion of Alphonse, Barbaroo, and Celeste is that this assumption is probably false. Moreover, and more to the present point, even when one of the desires, beliefs, and dispositions whose interplay gives rise to a person's bad act is itself bad, anyone who takes its badness to be what justifies us in condemning the agent will in effect be transforming the current proposal into a variant of Hume's—a transformation that will invite a variant of my now-familiar objection to the Humean view.

To see how that objection would work, suppose that what justified us in condemning someone who acted badly were precisely the badness of some element—call it e—of the larger complex, C, of desires, beliefs, and fine-grained dispositions whose interaction gave rise to his decision to perform the bad act. If our basis for condemning the agent were simply e's badness, then we would now have exactly the same basis for condemning him if C's bad element e were present but some other element of C were absent. We also would have the same basis for condemning him if all the elements of C including e were present but some crucial external factor—for example, the proximity of a vulnerable child—were absent. Yet if the element of C that provided our basis for condemning the agent could thus be detached from the other necessary conditions for his acting badly, then he would remain worthy of our condemnation even if he had not acted badly, and so his actually having acted badly would be no part of our basis for condemning him. Hence, on this account, the current proposal, like Hume's, would fail to explain why we are justified in condemning people for what they actually do.

Yet if it is not the badness of any operative element of an agent's character that justifies us in condemning him when he acts badly, then just how does the introduction of his desires, beliefs, and fine-grained dispositions advance the discussion? One thing this clearly makes possible is a more realistic account of the ways in which an agent's character can contribute to his acting badly. Instead of relying on Campbell's stylized contrast between the blandishments of inclination and the call of duty, we can now acknowledge that the crucial lapse can occur at any number of other points—for example, when the agent consciously decides to ignore his nagging doubts, when he fails to notice some morally relevant feature of his situation, or when he reasons in his usual slipshod manner.

Yet this acknowledgement, though correct and important, does not alter the central fact that wherever the fateful lapse occurs, it remains no less distinct from the agent himself than is the larger act for whose badness it is the fulcrum. Thus, our original question—why is it reasonable to condemn an agent when he acts badly?—seems yet again to reappear, this time as the question of why it is reasonable to condemn a person when some event in his decision-making process issues in his acting badly.

This, of course, is not good news for my proposal; for it suggests that despite the proposal's added complexity, we still face the same dilemma that we encountered above. Reduced to its essentials, the dilemma is that if something bad about an agent is what gives us reason to condemn him when he acts badly, then that something would give us no less reason to condemn him if it were present but the bad act itself absent; while if nothing bad about the agent gives us reason to condemn him when he acts badly, then although only the badness of the act itself is left to fill that role, the way in which the act's badness might do this remains a mystery. If my proposal cannot resolve this dilemma, it will represent no real improvement over the proposals of Hume and Campbell.

III

But although it is clear enough that any attempt to ground our condemnation of an agent who acts badly in the badness of any of his desires, beliefs, or dispositions would again embroil us in Hume's error, it is far less clear that every other possible way of invoking those desires, beliefs, and dispositions is bound to replicate Campbell's explanatory failure. Because their introduction adds a new layer of structure, they provide us with new resources that are unavailable to Campbell—resources I now want to exploit.[3] Put most simply, the crucial fact about the wrongdoer's desires, beliefs, and fine-grained dispositions is that they are strategically located between him and the badness of what he does. They are strategically located not merely in the weak sense that they are causal links in a sequence that extends from him *to* the bad act, but also in the stronger sense that they are intimately bound up with his identity on the one hand and with his doing what he has compelling moral reason not to do on the other. As an aggregate, they combine to make him the person he is, while through their interaction, they give rise to his failure to act as he should. Although each relation obviously raises many questions, we need not answer those questions to see that both relations go very deep.

And because they do, it is natural to entertain the thought that what justifies us in condemning an agent for the badness of what he does is precisely that his doing it is a joint product of the same attitudes

---

3. Because I agree that the only thing whose badness is relevant to our condemnation of a wrongdoer is his act itself, yet want to deny that this prevents us from explaining *why* we have reason to condemn him, my strategy will in effect be to attack the dilemma at its second horn.

and tendencies that also make him the person he is. By thus tracing the features of the act that make it bad to the interaction of a number of desires, beliefs, and dispositions, none of which need itself be bad, we may hope to avoid the objection that what justifies us in condemning the agent is something that would equally well justify us in condemning him if he did not act badly; while by demonstrating that the same desires, beliefs, and dispositions that collectively give rise to the act's badness are in addition collectively crucial to the agent's identity, we may also hope to establish the needed link between his act's badness and him.

Can this proposal be sustained? Can our rationale for condemning someone for acting badly really be that the action's bad-making features can be traced to the interplay of the same desires, beliefs, and dispositions that also make him the person he is? To make this claim plausible, I must say more both about how the features of an act that make it bad can emerge from the interplay of a variety of desires, beliefs, and fine-grained dispositions, none of which are themselves bad, and about how those desires, beliefs, and dispositions are in turn related to the agent's identity. These, accordingly, are my next topics.

IV

By introducing Alphonse, Barbaroo, and Celeste, I have already provided some illustration of my claim that an act's bad-making features can emerge from the interaction of various elements of the agent's character, none of which is itself bad. However, these examples were hastily sketched, and so are bound to leave various questions unanswered. Also, Alphonse, Barbaroo, and Celeste are hardly typical wrongdoers: each is a far better person than the average blameworthy agent. For both reasons, I now want to look in some detail at a new and more representative specimen—a kind of generic everywrongdoer.

Consider, in this regard, Ernie, a small-time criminal whom we encounter in the process of robbing a convenience store. Ernie's aim in robbing the store, we may suppose, is entirely pedestrian: he simply wants some money and believes that robbery is the easiest way to get it. This desire/belief pair is, in one instantly recognizable sense, his reason for robbing the store. Because robbing stores is morally forbidden, it is evidently possible to have a reason of this sort for doing something that one has a compelling *moral* reason *not* to do. To capture this distinction, I shall, following Thomas Scanlon, refer to the reasons that count for and against the acts available to an agent—the reasons by which he ought to be moved when on balance they favor some available action—as his *normative reasons,* and the reasons by which the agent is in fact moved as his *operative reasons.*[4]

Redescribed in these terms, Ernie is someone who has an operative reason for doing something that he has a compelling (moral) normative reason not to do. As we just saw, his operative reason has a desire/belief pair built right into it. Because of this, and because there is nothing morally wrong with either wanting money or with believing that robbery is the easiest way to get it, there is a minimal sense in which we are already entitled to say that Ernie's acting badly is rooted in a subset of his desires, beliefs, and dispositions, none of which is itself bad.

However, this minimal version of the claim is in itself too weak to sustain my argument. One reason it is too weak is that the cited desire/belief pair is far too insubstantial to have much to do with Ernie's identity. He would hardly become a different person if, distracted by romance, he ceased to care about money or if, having learned that he was to inherit a fortune, he ceased to regard robbery as the easiest route to wealth. In addition, if we considered only this single desire/belief pair, we would not do justice to the complexities even of Ernie's maximally simple transgression; and neither, therefore, would we effectively preclude the possibility that a fuller description *would* make essential reference to the badness of some relevant desire, belief, or disposition. For both reasons, we must now review the other main ways in which Ernie's desires, beliefs, and dispositions are apt to be implicated in the badness of what he does. I can think of at least five.

1. As just described, Ernie's reason for robbing the store is simply that he wants some money and believes that robbery is the easiest way to get it. However, even if someone has both this desire and this belief, he

4. These useful terms are introduced in Thomas Scanlon, *What We Owe to Each Other* (Cambridge, Mass.: Harvard University Press, 1998), 18–22.

is unlikely to rob a store if he also believes that most robbers are eventually caught and punished or that there are more attractive ways of getting money. In addition, someone with the cited desire/belief pair is unlikely to commit a robbery if he takes pride in working for a living or if he fears parental disapproval or divine retribution. Thus, if Ernie's operative reason is to include the relevant desire/belief pair, it will also have to include whichever of his other beliefs and desires preclude these possibilities—his beliefs that he probably won't be caught and that no better opportunities are available, his desire to avoid work, and so on.

2. Even by themselves, these considerations suggest that Ernie's operative reason is bound to encompass many beliefs and desires that extend well beyond the initial pair. However, that suggestion draws additional support from the fact that at least some of the relevant beliefs and desires are *themselves* likely to be based on reasons. For example, Ernie's reason for believing that he won't be caught may include his further beliefs that the area is lightly patrolled and that the police are inept; while his reason for wanting money may be that he wants to buy drugs and impress his friends. Because each sequence of sustaining reasons can obviously extend further, some elements of some sequences may be too remote from Ernie's decision to qualify as constituents of his operative reason. However, what matters for present purposes is not that some outliers may not qualify but that many intermediate elements apparently do. For example, once we acknowledge that Ernie's operative reason includes his belief that he probably won't be caught, there is little point in denying that it also includes his beliefs that the area is lightly patrolled and that the police are inept.

3. Whenever someone believes p because he believes q, his believing q is part of the cause of his believing p; and the same holds, *mutatis mutandis*, for someone's wanting A because he wants B. Thus, even if some of the desires and beliefs that support the desires and beliefs on the basis of which Ernie acts are too remote from his action to qualify as constituents *of* his operative reason, they are all direct or indirect causal contributors to it. Because none of Ernie's beliefs or desires are too remote from his action to have the latter status, the number of his beliefs and desires that contribute causally to his operative reason is apt to be considerably larger than the number that enter as its constituents.

4. Moreover, just as an indefinitely large subset of Ernie's background beliefs and desires may contribute causally to his operative

reason, so, too, may an indefinitely large subset of his fine-grained dispositions. For every belief or desire in the absence of which Ernie would not act as he does, he is bound to have many tendencies to classify, feel, and infer in the absence of which he would not have that belief or desire. These causally relevant dispositions are likely to include many tendencies that we can name—for example, Ernie's impulsiveness, his intellectual laziness, his quickness to rationalize, and his defensiveness about not having marketable skills—but they are also bound to include countless other tendencies that are far too delicate to categorize, yet whose interaction is precisely what determines what Ernie finds salient or plausible or attractive or intolerable at any given moment. It is, of course, just the latter tendencies that we painstakingly disentangle in the process of coming to know others (and ourselves) better.

5. Because Ernie's action is one that morality gives him a compelling normative reason not to perform, there is a sense in which anything that contributes to any constituent of his operative reason for performing it must also contribute to his failure to act as morality requires. That is why the previous four paragraphs were relevant. Nevertheless, it is one thing to say that some of Ernie's desires, beliefs, and dispositions contribute to his failure to act as morality requires by causally sustaining (or being) his operative reason for acting as he does, and quite another to say that some of them contribute by preventing him from acquiring other desires or beliefs—for example, a belief that stealing is wrong or a desire not to do what is wrong—which, if he had them, would be constituents or causes of an alternative operative reason *for* acting as morality requires. Because it is precisely Ernie's failure to be moved by the wrongness of stealing that renders his act bad, my argument would be greatly strengthened if his desires, beliefs, and dispositions could also be shown to contribute to its badness in the latter way.

And so, in fact, they can; for when someone fails to recognize or respond to a given moral reason, that failure, too, can standardly be traced to one or another subset of his desires, beliefs, and dispositions. For example, when Ernie is unmoved by the wrongness of stealing, one possible explanation is that some other strong desire or tendency—a craving for the approval of his friends, say, or a tendency to panic when forced to make a quick decision—has temporarily distracted him from his desire to avoid wrongdoing. Another possible explanation is that

Ernie holds certain false moral beliefs—for example, that merchants are oppressors to whom no moral duties are owed—from which he infers that robbing stores is *not* wrong. Yet a third possibility is that he lacks some capacity—for example, to imagine the reality of others or to feel bad at the thought of their feeling bad—which is a prerequisite for taking morality seriously. And, of course, it is clear both that there are many other possibilities and that a fuller elaboration of each possibility would disclose yet another web of supporting desires, beliefs, and dispositions.

Even as augmented, this account remains very sketchy. Nevertheless, it is detailed enough to suggest that even the simplest of transgressions—and Ernie's is as simple as they come—is bound to be rooted in a large and wide-ranging subset of the agent's desires, beliefs, and dispositions. Moreover, although we have seen that the relevant desires, beliefs, and dispositions may indeed include some elements that are themselves bad—it is, for example, clearly bad to be insensitive to the feelings of others—we also saw that there are many scenarios in which each is neutral or better. Thus, the first of the two claims I said I needed to establish—that whenever someone acts badly, his act's bad-making features can be traced to the interaction of a significant subset of his desires, beliefs, and dispositions, none of which need itself be bad—appears secure.

V

But what next, of my second claim, that the same desires, beliefs, and dispositions whose interaction gives rise to the bad-making features of a person's act are also crucially implicated in his identity? That claim, too, is essential to my argument, since without it I will not be able to establish the needed linkage between the act's badness and the agent himself. Hence, to complete my argument, I must now defend this further claim.

That would be a daunting task if establishing the linkage meant refuting every theory of the self that does not simply identify the person with his desires, beliefs, and dispositions. However, when we survey the alternatives, we quickly discover that each additional necessary condition for personhood—the possession of a human body, for example, or the presence of an underlying mental substance—is standardly introduced either to account for the person's continued existence as his desires, beliefs, and dispositions change, or else to explain why each of these psychological states belongs to the same "bundle." Of these further aims, neither would be intelligible if we did not suppose that some or all of the person's desires, beliefs, and dispositions do play a crucial role in making him the person he is. Thus, even among these more elaborate theories, the contributions of a person's psychological states to his identity not only are common ground, but also retain a certain priority.

And this is hardly surprising in light of the connection between being a person and having the capacity to engage in activities that *require* a complex psychology. As Locke pointed out in the *Essay Concerning Human Understanding*, "person," unlike "human being," "is a forensic term, appropriating actions and their merit; and so belongs only to intelligent agents, capable of a law, and happiness, and misery."[5] Because any person must have the kind of psychology that only a highly complex and integrated set of desires, beliefs, and dispositions can make possible—because a being that lacked such a psychology would simply not be a person—it is only to be expected that which person one is will depend crucially on which desires, beliefs, and dispositions one has.

In saying this, I mean to take no position in the dispute between those who view all aspects of a person's psychology as relevant to his identity and those others who believe that only some of them are relevant. Of those who hold the latter view, some maintain that a person's identity is determined exclusively by those desires that he wants to have and by which he wants to be motivated, while others give priority to those desires, beliefs, and dispositions that he endorses or that express his values. If someone holds any version of this view, to which Susan Wolf has usefully referred as "the real self view,"[6] then he will believe

5. John Locke, *An Essay Concerning Human Understanding*, ed. Alexander Campbell Fraser (New York: Dover, 1959), vol. 1, book II, chap. XXVII, 467.

6. Wolf introduces this designation in her book *Freedom Within Reason* (New York: Oxford University Press, 1990). For two important variants of the view, see Harry Frankfurt, "Freedom of the Will and the Concept of a Person," in Harry Frankfurt, *The Importance of What We Care About* (Cambridge: Cambridge University Press, 1988), 11–25, and Gary Watson, "Free Agency," *The Journal of Philosophy* 72 (April 24, 1975): 205–20. For critical discussion, see Nomy Arpaly and Timothy Schroeder, "Praise, Blame, and the Whole Self," *Philosophical Studies* 93 (February 1999): 162–88.

that some bad acts, such as those of addicts and kleptomaniacs, originate in impulses that are too alien to the agent to support my explanation of why it is reasonable to condemn him. However, because the point of introducing the real self view is often precisely to *account for* the intuition that addicts, kleptomaniacs, and the like are not blameworthy, this implication hardly threatens my account.

Hence, for present purposes, we need not choose between the real self view and its more inclusive rival. As long as we restrict our attention to those acts that intuitively *do* render agents blameworthy, both views are equally capable of supporting the inference from the premise that an act's badness can be traced to the interaction of a large and wide-ranging subset of the agent's desires, beliefs, and dispositions to the conclusion that the act's badness can be attributed to the agent himself.

VI

This completes my explanation of why it is reasonable to condemn an agent when he acts badly. Like Hume, I have appealed to certain facts about the agent's character; but unlike Hume, I do not take these to include the fact that his character is bad.[7] By invoking only the badness of the act itself, I have tried to block the implication that we would be

---

7. Because my explanation appeals only to those fine-grained dispositions that interact with an agent's desires and beliefs and each other to give rise to his bad acts, it could survive a demonstration that such dispositions are the only kind there are. For an argument that there are no broad-based dispositions of the kind that we associate with character traits, see Gilbert Harman, "Moral Philosophy Meets Social Psychology: Virtue Ethics and the Fundamental Attribution Error," *Proceedings of the Aristotelian Society,* New Series XCIX, part 3 (1999): 315–31. However, for a more cautious (and I think more plausible) reading of the data to which Harman appeals, see John Doris, *Lack of Character* (Cambridge: Cambridge University Press, 2002). On Doris's reading, what the data show is only that vices and virtues that are robust enough to satisfy my BC1 are far less common than most of us believe: "the situationist does not deny the existence of monsters, but she does deny that the explanation of their behavior will be applicable to the generality of cases" (p. 55). This seems consistent with the claim that what I have called character flaws—that is, dispositions to act badly under a broad enough range of conditions to satisfy BC2—are very common.

no less justified in condemning the agent if he had the same bad character but lacked the opportunity to manifest it by acting badly.

But have I in fact blocked this implication? In the previous chapter, I remarked that because the bad acts of Alphonse, Barbaroo, and Celeste can be traced to the interaction of some of their desires, beliefs, and fine-grained dispositions with some aspects of their situations, each when he acts must be disposed to perform acts of precisely that sort in precisely that situation. By the same token, if Ernie's desires, beliefs, and dispositions interact with aspects of his situation to give rise to his robbery, then he, too, must then be disposed to rob stores in situations exactly like the one that prevails. But isn't this disposition itself both a bad aspect of Ernie's character and a feature he would have whether or not there were a store to rob? And, hence, doesn't my own account share with Hume's the implication that we would be no less justified in condemning Ernie if he had the same character but had no opportunity to rob a store?

I clearly must concede that Ernie's robbing the store is a manifestation of a (perhaps only momentary) disposition to rob stores in situations like the one that prevails. I am also willing to concede that Ernie's having this disposition is a bad feature of his character and that he would have it even if there were no store to rob. Moreover, although the argument remains to be made, I believe that defects of character can indeed render agents blameworthy. However, even together, these concessions do not show that my account either collapses into Hume's or is rendered superfluous by a variant of it.

The reason my account remains non-Humean is that whereas Hume's account takes what is bad about Ernie's character to be the very thing we are justified in condemning him for, my own account treats the relevant bad aspect of his character—his disposition to rob stores under just the conditions that prevail—as merely an incidental consequence of his having the vastly broader combination of desires, beliefs, and dispositions that links him to the actual robbery whose badness *in turn* makes it reasonable to condemn him. On my account but not Hume's, the act's badness remains an independent basis upon which we can legitimately condemn the agent. Because of this, my own account, unlike Hume's, remains able to capture the crucial thought that our grounds for condemning Ernie include his actual flouting of a moral requirement.

Because my account makes essential reference to the badness of the actual robbery, its implication that Ernie has a disposition that is also to a degree bad, and for which he may also deserve some blame, does not make it a variant of Hume's. But that implication might still be thought to undermine my account in a different way—namely, by showing it to be redundant. For if every bad act does manifest a disposition that itself renders the agent blameworthy, then won't the most economical explanation of why we are justified in blaming wrongdoers be one that appeals exclusively to their bad dispositions? And, hence, even if my account does not collapse into Hume's, won't the ubiquitous availability of the Humean account end by rendering mine superfluous?

This objection would have considerable force if the Humean account were even roughly adequate. However, the central thrust of the previous chapter was precisely that it is not. Thus, to disarm the objection, I need only repeat two points that have already been made. The first point is that if we take our basis for condemning a wrongdoer to be simply the badness of his character, then we will not be able to explain why it is reasonable to condemn someone like Donato for his particular act of taunting the child. The second is that if we take a wrongdoer's degree of blameworthiness to depend on the breadth of his disposition to act badly, then we will grossly understate the blameworthiness of someone like Alphonse, whose disposition to act cruelly is very narrow but who nevertheless remains highly blameworthy for viciously humiliating his vulnerable student on a single occasion.

Even by themselves, these considerations would show that the proposed account is far from superfluous. However, in fact, there is more to be said. Just as Hume's account often understates the blameworthiness of good people who do bad things, it often *over*states the blameworthiness of *bad* people who do bad things. To bring this out, and thus to highlight a further respect in which my own proposal is preferable, I must bring Donato back for one final curtain call.

Donato, we saw, is thoroughly cruel. He is disposed to act in ways that cause others to suffer, and to enjoy their suffering, under a very broad range of conditions. Thus, if what determined how blameworthy Donato is when he taunts the child were simply the breadth of his disposition to act cruelly, then it would follow that he is very blameworthy indeed. But is this necessarily true? Suppose we elaborate the case by adding that the child's parents, who have long harbored suspicions about Donato, are hovering vigilantly nearby; and suppose we say that Donato therefore can do nothing worse than leaving one of the child's toys just out of reach in its crib. If Donato's opportunities for cruelty are thus constrained—if he is forced to settle for a bit of nasty teasing—then his taunting, though indeed blameworthy, will simply not be serious enough to warrant strong condemnation. Hence, in this variant of the case, the Humean account will imply that Donato is far more blameworthy than he actually is.

My own account, by contrast, makes it clear both why Donato can reasonably be blamed for (what has now become) his minor act of taunting and why the condemnation he deserves is relatively mild. Simply put, the reason we may condemn Donato for taunting the child is that this act, like Ernie's robbery and the cruel behavior of Alphonse, Barbaroo, and Celeste, is at once forbidden by morality and traceable to the interaction of a complex subset of the desires, beliefs, and fine-grained dispositions that together make their possessor the person he is. However, because the prohibition against malicious teasing is, in a familiar but elusive sense that I shall not attempt to specify, far less stringent than the prohibitions against either tormenting unhappy souls or robbing stores, the condemnation that Donato deserves is relatively mild. In Donato's case, of course, the taunting is most directly trace-able not to the interaction of a variety of fine-grained dispositions but rather to a single coarse-grained disposition to act cruelly under a broad range of conditions. However, to square this with the pattern I have sketched, we need only note that Donato's coarse-grained disposition is itself likely to be rooted in certain stable patterns of interaction among his desires, beliefs, and finer-grained dispositions.

The only remaining question, therefore, is whether Donato's dis-position to act cruelly under a broad range of conditions—the cruelty that pervades his character—is a further basis upon which we may reasonably condemn him. Can we blame him for being cruel *as well as* for behaving cruelly? As I have already intimated, I think the claim that people can reasonably be blamed for their moral vices is the second main element of truth in the Humean account. However, many would reject this claim on the grounds that most people have exercised far too little control over their characters to deserve any blame for them. Thus, before we can evaluate the claim that people can be blamed for their bad traits as well as their bad acts, we will have to look more carefully at the relation between blame and control.

FOUR

BLAME FOR TRAITS

DESPITE THEIR EFFORTS TO REDIRECT OUR BLAME FROM BAD ACTS TO THE BAD traits they manifest, neither Hume nor his followers have said much in defense of the assumption that traits are an appropriate basis for blame. This omission is striking because the assumption is controversial: many would reject it on the grounds that our traits are largely beyond our control. However, in the current chapter, I will argue that blame for traits (henceforth BFT) can indeed be defended. Although I do not agree that people cannot be blamed for their bad acts, I do think their bad traits provide an independent and free-standing class of reasons to blame them.

I

The standard anti-BFT argument asserts that:

1. no one deserves blame for anything beyond his control and
2. people generally lack control over their bad traits, so
3. people generally deserve no blame for their bad traits.

Although this argument is not universally accepted, there is wide agreement that its first premise is beyond dispute. Given the near-consensus on this point, the argument's opponents—an unlikely coalition of

Aristotelians and Kantians—usually direct their fire at (2). Against this premise, they argue that when we widen our scope to encompass the earlier decisions that causally contributed to the development of people's bad traits, we discover that many of those traits once were (and so, for moral purposes, can still be treated as) within their possessors' control.[1]

It seems to me, however, that this approach is doubly misguided—that premise (2) is far more plausible, and premise (1) far less so, than these critics have recognized. Consequently, my own approach to the anti-BFT argument will be the reverse of theirs. I will accept (2)'s claim that most bad people cannot help being the way they are, but will reject (1)'s contention that this lack of control renders it inappropriate to blame them for being the way they are. This departure from the usual approach will yield a version of BFT that is not restricted to the tame assertion that bad people can be blamed for failing to prevent themselves from becoming bad, but rather makes the more interesting claim that bad people can be blamed simply for being bad.

Let me begin with my reasons for accepting (2). When I say that (most) bad people have exercised little control over the development of their bad traits, I do not mean to deny that there often were steps that, had those people previously taken them, would have caused them not to become bad. If character is malleable at all, then such steps probably often were available. However, even where they were, we cannot infer that those who are now bad were ever in control of the processes through which they became bad. To see why this inference fails, we need only remind ourselves of what, beyond having the bare ability to do something that would prevent a bad outcome, having effective control over that outcome involves.

1. For two typical challenges to (2), see Michele Moody-Adams, "On the Old Saw That Character Is Destiny," in *Identity, Character, and Morality,* ed. Owen Flanagan and Amelie Oksenberg Rorty (Cambridge, Mass.: MIT Press, 1990), 111–31, and Marcia Baron, *Kantian Ethics Almost Without Apology* (Ithaca, N.Y.: Cornell University Press, 1995), 76–77 and *passim.* For a defense of BFT that atypically challenges (1) rather than (2), see Robert Merrihew Adams, "Involuntary Sins," *The Philosophical Review* XCIV (January 1985): 3–31.

Control has both an epistemic and a volitional component. To exercise control over a given outcome, an agent must know both how to bring it about and how to prevent it, and must in addition be capable of bending his will in either direction. Corresponding to these two aspects of control, there are two broad necessary conditions for its effective exercise.

To specify the exact content of the epistemic condition, we would have to go into considerable detail about how conscious, how detailed, and how well grounded the controlling agent's beliefs about his situation must be. However, to bring out what is wrong with (2), we need not operate at this level of detail. For our purposes, it is enough to note that even when someone is able to do something that in fact would prevent a bad outcome, he lacks effective control over that outcome if he neither has any idea of how to prevent it nor has any other knowledge from which this could reasonably be inferred. For example, although the physicians of the fourteenth century were physically able to do many things that would have slowed the spread of the Black Plague—they could have burned the bedding of plague victims, killed rats, or taken other sanitary measures—they had no idea how the disease was transmitted, and so could not know that those steps would have the desired effect. Because the fourteenth-century physicians lacked this knowledge, they lacked effective control over the plague.

Given the obscurity that surrounds the notion of will, the other necessary condition for control—the requirement that the agent be able to bend his will in either direction—seems if anything to be even less straightforward than its epistemic counterpart. However, here again, we need not go into detail: for our purposes, what matters is simply that control drops off drastically once the difficulty of doing something reaches a certain level. An agent may lack effective control over a bad outcome not only because he is physically incapable of preventing it, but also because the only available course of action is so demanding as to require a heroic exercise of will. This necessary condition is violated when the only way to save a life—one's own or another's—is to cut off one's leg without anesthesia. Less dramatically, it may be violated when someone with acrophobia must climb a tree to save his cat. In general, a person can be said to lack effective control over a bad outcome whenever preventing it would require a greater effort of will than he can reasonably be expected to make.[2]

Bearing these necessary conditions in mind, let us return to the person with the bad character; and let us ask how likely it is that he ever had effective control over the development of his bad traits. The crucial question, we can now see, is whether such a person could ever reasonably have been expected to (a) believe that certain actions would prevent the development of what are now his vices, and (b) perform those actions. Moreover, when the question is put this way, we can quickly see why its answer is very often "no."

For, first, a child's character is malleable as an adult's is not, so much of what can be done to prevent a person from developing bad traits must be done when he is young. However, an immature, unformed agent is unlikely either to know much about what he must do to become a good person or to care much about doing it. Thus, whether a child's character develops in the right way depends largely on whether he is lucky enough to receive a sound moral education. If he is not, we can hardly blame him for not seeking one out. Even when a child is able to do various things that would in fact result in his receiving the requisite moral instruction—even when, for example, it is within his power to study a simplified version of Aristotle's ethics or talk his way into a military academy—these are not steps that someone whose picture of the world is not yet formed, and who has had little experience or guidance, can reasonably be expected to take.

Thus, if someone whose character is now bad could ever reasonably have been expected to take steps to prevent his own corruption,

---

2. In specifying the volitional condition for control in this way, I mean to sidestep the question of whether universal causation itself deprives us of every option but one. One reason we need not address that question is that the truth of hard determinism would imply that we never exercised control over either our actions *or* our traits, and so would not be capable of sustaining a targeted attack on BFT. A further reason for disregarding it is that the anti-BFT argument that we are considering is endorsed by many compatibilists as well as many incompatibilists, and so must be reconstructed in a way that both sides can accept. For both reasons, I will not consider the dispute over "alternative possibilities" further. For a sampling of the large literature on this topic, see *Moral Responsibility*, ed. John Martin Fischer (Ithaca, N.Y.: Cornell University Press, 1986), part II.

the time at which this expectation was reasonable could not have come until after he had achieved a degree of maturity. However, by that time, the person's bad traits were already partly in place, and so the task was obviously much harder. It is far more difficult to undo a vice than to prevent its development. There are, of course, various techniques that someone who wants to become a better person can use. He can, for example, reflect on his past lapses, force himself to do what does not (yet) come naturally, imitate exemplary others, and avoid those whom he knows to be bad influences. However, such techniques are only effective when they are employed regularly and conscientiously and are often ineffective even then. Thus, by the time a miscreant-in-training has already achieved a degree of maturity, the expectation that he will display the insight, flexibility, and persistence that are needed to arrest or reverse his incipient corruption may well be unreasonable.

Because so many bad traits have developed through processes that their possessors could not reasonably have been expected to prevent (and because there is usually no way of telling which bad traits a person could reasonably have been expected to prevent), we cannot simultaneously hold both that people deserve blame only for the bad traits over whose development they once exercised control and that they deserve blame for all, or even most, of their bad traits. And, for this reason, anyone who wishes to defeat the anti-BFT argument must indeed do so by rebutting (1). He must show that despite initial appearances, it is false that no one deserves blame for anything he cannot help. But is it really plausible to reject this widely accepted claim?

II

To find out, we must look more carefully at the reasons for (1)'s appeal. There are, I think, two main considerations that tell in (1)'s favor: first, that it seems to account for certain intuitions that we would be very reluctant to abandon, and, second, that it seems to follow from a widely accepted principle of fairness. Thus, to show that we may legitimately reject (1), I will have to establish that neither consideration is decisive.

There is universal agreement that we cannot blame people for many of the acts and omissions over which they lack control. For example, we clearly cannot blame either a driver who injures a pedestrian because his brakes have failed or a friend who misses an appointment because his bus is late. It is no less universally agreed that we cannot blame people for their physical or mental defects—for being clumsy or ugly or stupid, for example. These facts seem relevant to (1) because they all appear to be explained by, and thus to confirm, (1)'s claim that no one deserves blame for anything he cannot help. If this explanation were correct, then any defense of BFT that required that we reject (1) would also imply that we must revise our intuitions about such cases— an implication that would amount to a *reductio* of the proposed defense.

But I want to argue that the proposed explanation is *not* correct, and that to whatever extent it is true that we cannot blame people for acts or omissions that they cannot help, or for their physical or mental defects, the reasons for this are quite independent of (1).[3] To show this, I will propose alternative explanations of both intuitions. Because my alternative explanation of why we cannot blame a person for an act or omission that is beyond his control is quite different from my alternative explanation of why we cannot blame a person for his physical or mental defects, I will have to consider each type of case separately.

To see how there might be an alternative explanation of our inability to blame people for acts or omissions that they cannot help, we must first note that a person's lack of control over what he does may figure in an explanation of our inability to blame him in either of two distinct ways. It may enter because control itself is a necessary condition for blame—this is what (1) says—but it may enter instead because exercising control over the relevant act or omission is necessary for the

---

3. My reason for using the hedging expression "to whatever extent it is true" is that on one common interpretation of the epistemic component of control, the claim that agents can only deserve blame for acts (or omissions) over which they have exercised control does *not* seem true. The interpretation that I have in mind is one that holds that exercising control over an outcome requires being consciously aware that one's act or omission will bring that outcome about. That people can deserve blame for acts or omissions over which they lack such control is suggested by our reactions to a case in which (e.g.) an agent causes a pet (or a child) to suffer heatstroke by forgetting that he has left the pet or child in a hot car. I discuss a number of examples of this sort in my paper "Out of Control," *Ethics* (forthcoming). However, in the current discussion, I will ignore this complication and simply accept the claim that it is never appropriate to blame an agent for an act or omission over which he lacks control.

satisfaction of some further condition that in its turn is necessary for blame. If an agent's lack of control over his act or omission enters only in this second way, then the resulting explanation of why his lack of control renders blame inappropriate may not apply to persons whose bad *traits* are beyond their control; for even if a bad act can only satisfy the real necessary condition for blame by falling within the agent's control, a bad trait may be able to satisfy it in some quite different way.

And, in fact, this is no mere idle possibility; for to arrive at a necessary condition for blame whose satisfaction requires control in the case of acts but not traits, we need only recall a truism that we encountered in the previous chapter. The truism that I have in mind is that blaming a person for something involves taking its moral defects to reflect badly on him; and the corresponding necessary condition is that no one can deserve blame for anything that does not stand in a close enough relation *to* him to reflect badly *on* him. In chapter 3, I argued that this necessary condition is satisfied whenever (a) an act is bad in the sense that the agent has failed to respond to some compelling moral reason for not performing it, and (b) the agent's failure to respond to that reason can be traced to the interaction of certain features of his situation with some significant subset of the desires, beliefs, and dispositions that together make him the person he is. To these claims, I now want to add, as my alternative explanation of why someone who lacks control over his wrong act does not deserve to be blamed for it, that whatever deprives an agent of control over his act must also render it false that the desires, beliefs, and dispositions that make him the person he is are the source of his failure to respond to the relevant moral reason.

To see how this explanation works, consider first a case in which an agent's lack of control over his act is due to ignorance—for example, a case in which an agent continues to drive because he does not know that his brakes are about to fail. In this case, the reason the driver is not acting badly is simply that he lacks access to the factual basis of his reason to stop driving. Because he is ignorant of the fact that gives him reason to stop driving, he is not in a position to recognize that reason, and neither, therefore, is he acting in a way that is unresponsive to it.

By contrast, if what deprives an agent of control over his act is the impossibility or inordinate difficulty of acting differently—if, for example, the agent is an addict or is in the grip of a (genuine) compulsion— then the explanation of why his failure to act for the relevant moral reasons does not reflect badly on him is different. Here the point is not that the agent's ignorance prevented him from responding to the relevant moral reason, but is rather that he lacks the capacity to translate his response into action. Even if he is admirably reason-responsive, there is, by hypothesis, still an unbridgeable gap between his reason-based desire to do the right thing and what he actually does.

When someone performs a wrong act over which he lacks control, the wrongness of what he does cannot be attributed to his failure to respond to the relevant moral reason. This explains why his act's wrongness does not cast a negative shadow on him. However, no comparable explanation can be given when a person has a bad trait over which he lacks control; for to have a bad trait just *is* to be systematically unresponsive to the corresponding class of moral reasons. A person who is duplicitous is systematically unresponsive to the reasons for telling the truth, a person who is cruel is systematically unresponsive to reasons not to hurt others, and so on. Even if the bad trait's possessor has never in fact failed to respond to any moral reason of the relevant sort, and even if his having that trait is due to no previous failure to respond to any other moral reason, it remains true that he would fail to respond to moral reasons of the relevant sort, and thus would act badly in the relevant sense, under a wide range of conditions. Because this bad disposition is itself an element of his character, it clearly does reflect badly on him. Thus, whenever someone is selfish or dishonest or cruel, the relevant necessary condition for blame is indeed met. This of course does not show that anyone *can* be blamed for having a bad trait—to establish that, I will need a positive argument of a kind that I have yet to produce—but it does show that we can explain why people cannot be blamed for acts over which they lack control without relying on any premise that would prevent us from accepting BFT.

What, next, of our inability to blame people for their physical or mental defects? Can we reject (1), and thus remove the main obstacle to blaming people for being cruel or selfish or dishonest, without opening up the possibility of blaming people for being clumsy or ugly or stupid as well? Can we also explain why it is inappropriate to blame people for the latter defects in a way that does not rely on (1)?

To see that we can, we need only remind ourselves of yet another truism—one that is, if anything, even more obvious than the truism that people can only be blamed for what reflects badly on them. This is the truism that moral blame—the kind we have been considering—can only be deserved for some kind of *moral* failing. This new necessary condition for blameworthiness is unproblematically satisfied by vices such as cruelty, selfishness, and dishonesty; for as we saw, the possessor of each such vice is systematically unresponsive to an important class of moral reasons. By contrast, and decisively, the new necessary condition is just as clearly *un*satisfied by defects such as clumsiness, ugliness, and stupidity. It is unsatisfied by clumsiness and ugliness because these defects do not affect a person's responsiveness to reasons at all; while it is unsatisfied by stupidity because although a lack of intelligence manifestly does affect the reasons to which a person can respond, stupidity seems compatible with virtually any degree of responsiveness to moral reasons. Because even very stupid people can be admirably sensitive to what morality requires,[4] a mere lack of intelligence is not (though it may of course be associated with) a moral failing that renders someone deserving of blame.[5]

Given all this, we need not worry that abandoning (1) will open the door to blaming people either for wrong acts that they cannot help performing or for merely undesirable traits. Of course, without further discussion, we cannot assume that even moral vices are proper occasions for blame; for nothing yet said shows that the moral failings for which people can be blamed include both bad traits *and* wrong acts. However, to point this out is only to reemphasize that I have not yet

---

4. Stupidity may on occasion render someone unable to appreciate the empirical facts upon which a given moral reason depends, but it does not appear to render anyone *systematically* insensitive to moral reasons.

5. Even if no one can deserve moral blame for anything except a moral failing, mightn't a nonmoral failing such as clumsiness or ugliness still render someone deserving of a response that was indistinguishable from blame in every respect except the nonmoral nature of its occasion? And, if so, then won't the objection under discussion—that if we reject (1), we will have to pay the price of admitting that people can be blamed for being clumsy or ugly or stupid as well as for being cruel or selfish or dishonest—remain substantially unmet? The answer, I think, is that the objection would remain unmet if the connection between blame and moral failure were merely definitional, but that in fact that connection is *not* merely definitional. As I will argue in the chapters that follow, the best integrated theory of blame and blameworthiness is one that takes a commitment to morality to lie at the very heart of both notions.

offered any positive argument for BFT. This is true, but it does not affect my present point, which is only that we can deny that control is a necessary condition for blame without having to accept any counter-intuitive implications.

III

Yet even so, many will insist that control is a necessary condition for blame; for this necessary condition is often thought to be a require-ment of fairness. Those who take this position are in effect appealing to a principle—call it F—that says that it is unfair to blame a person for anything he cannot help. Thus, the crucial question about their ar-gument is whether we should accept F.

This question is hard to answer because F has, to my knowledge, never been defended.[6] It is, moreover, not at all clear how F could *be* defended. Yet in the end this may not matter, since moral inquiry must come to an end somewhere and F is an obvious candidate for bedrock status. Or, if "bedrock" sounds too foundational, F may at least be one of the "provisional fixed points" of our considered moral judgments.[7] Like the views that suffering is bad and that each person has moral worth, the view that it is never fair to blame people for what they cannot help may at least be certain enough to serve as a touchstone in our quest for reflective equilibrium.

But, for two reasons, I doubt that even the weaker of these sug-gestions holds. My first reason for doubt is that intuitions about blame are curiously mixed. Although many do think it unfair to blame someone for what he cannot help, many others—and, indeed, many of

6. In *Responsibility and the Moral Sentiments* (Cambridge, Mass.: Harvard, 1994), R. Jay Wallace proposes two interpretations of the relevant notion of fairness, one in terms of desert, the other in terms of reasonableness; see pp. 103–09 and passim. Wallace does not, however, have much to say about the normative underpinnings of the relevant version of either notion. For a pessimistic assessment of the prospects for grounding F in any premises about what agents can reasonably be asked to do, see my "Kantian Fairness," *Philosophical Issues* (forthcoming).

7. See John Rawls, *A Theory of Justice* (Cambridge, Mass.: Harvard University Press, 1971), 20 and 48–51.

the same people—retain the urge to condemn a miscreant not only for specific acts of cruelty or injustice, but also for the enduring cast of mind that gives rise to these. Of course, by itself, this ambivalence proves little, since the urge to blame people for their bad traits may be as irrational and atavistic as (say) the desire for revenge is often said to be. However, another possibility, which also must be kept open, is that this urge does have a sound rational basis from which we are often diverted by seductive but misleading analogies or arguments.[8] If we simply assume F from the outset, we will prematurely foreclose the latter possibility.

Moreover—and this is my second reason for not wanting to assign F a privileged status—there is, on reflection, a good deal that can be said against F. The basic source of the difficulty is that many of the acts over which agents exercise control are themselves manifestations of *traits* over which they *lack* control. When someone performs such an act, his control over it may not go very deep. If it does not, then we may wonder whether it is any fairer to blame him for manifesting his bad trait than merely for having it. If there is no difference in fairness, then anyone who insists that it is not unfair to blame an agent for such an act will indeed have to reject F.

I must emphasize that what is at issue is not whether anyone *can* exercise control over a bad act without also exercising control over any bad traits the act manifests—on any reasonable account of what it is to exercise control over an act, this does seem possible—but is only whether exercising control over acts under these conditions is morally significant. And, on inspection, that seems to depend on how closely the bad act over which the agent exercises control is connected to the bad traits over which he lacks it. Roughly speaking, the more nearly inevitable an agent's bad traits render his bad acts, the less plausible it is to say that we can fairly blame him for performing the acts but not for having the traits.

The crucial question, therefore, is how close to inevitable a person's bad traits do render his bad acts; and to this question, the only accurate answer is "it varies." At one end of the spectrum, we find cases in which the relation between a bad trait and its manifestation in

---

8. I think, in fact, that something like this may also be also true of the desire for revenge; for some details, see the essay "Deserved Punishment Revisited" in my *Approximate Justice: Studies in Non-Ideal Theory* (Lanham, Md.: Rowman and Littlefield, 1997), 165–80.

action is very loose—a case, for example, in which someone's envy or cruelty gives rise to a malicious desire that, when it comes time to act, he simply chooses not to resist. Somewhat less clear-cut, but still involving a substantial element of choice, is a case in which an agent's decision not to resist his envy-driven malicious impulse is abetted by a rationalization that is itself rooted in envy.[9] Still more nearly automatic are choices among alternatives whose very framing is somehow influenced by the agent's bad character—for example, a case in which a selfish person's insensitivity to the needs of others causes him not to bring into clear focus, or not to take as seriously as he should, the option of helping someone else at some cost to himself.[10] And still further toward the automatic end of the spectrum are the bad acts that agents perform because they are so corrupt that doing the right thing never even makes it onto their radar screen. As a small-scale example of this, we may imagine someone who steals whenever he can get away with it because he simply sees no point in being honest; for larger-scale examples, we may look to the world's Hitlers and Stalins.[11]

9. For discussion of a case with a similar structure, see James Wallace, *Virtues and Vices* (Ithaca, N.Y.: Cornell University Press, 1978), 67–74.

10. Compare John McDowell: "A kind person has a reliable sensitivity to a certain sort of requirement which situations impose on behavior" (John McDowell, "Virtue and Reason," in *Virtue Ethics*, ed. Roger Crisp and Michael Slote [Oxford: Oxford University Press, 1997], 142). For related discussion, see Lawrence Blum's "Moral Perception and Particularity" in his *Moral Perception and Particularity* (Cambridge: Cambridge University Press, 1994), 30–61; Martha C. Nussbaum, "The Discernment of Perception: An Aristotelian Conception of Public and Private Rationality" in her *Love's Knowledge: Essays on Philosophy and Literature* (New York: Oxford University Press, 1990), 54–105; and Nancy Sherman, *The Fabric of Character* (Oxford: Oxford University Press, 1989), 13–55.

11. When I say that many bad acts are rendered (near-)inevitable by the agents' bad traits, I do not mean to suggest either that these acts are performed in a mechanical fashion or that they are not preceded by careful deliberation. Even someone whose dominant trait is avarice, and who therefore sees the misfortunes of others simply as so many occasions for financial gain, may think long and hard about how to exploit a given opportunity. The point, rather, is that if what he deliberates about is only how to exploit another's plight effectively, then the operative option-range is restricted to actions any of which would be bad. Thus, strictly speaking, what the agent's bad character renders (near-)inevitable is not his performance of any particular bad act, but only his doing *something* bad.

How does this continuum affect the case against F? The answer, I think, is that it provides that case with substantial support; for as long as any significant number of bad acts are rendered (close to) inevitable by the corresponding traits, there will remain a significant class of agents whom we cannot fairly blame for their bad acts without also blaming them for their bad traits. Thus, as long as we can fairly blame people for bad acts that are the near-inevitable effects of their bad traits, there will be no shortage of counterexamples to F.

And, in fact, blaming people for such bad acts often does seem fair. At a minimum, it appears no less fair to blame someone for a bad act that he performs because he is so selfish that the suffering of others barely registers on his consciousness, or because he is so corrupt that he sees no point in being honest, than it does to blame another who sees the point of being honest perfectly well, but who decides — perhaps after a struggle — to give in to a dishonest impulse. Indeed, if anything, many would actually consider it fairer to blame the thoroughly corrupt person, whose bad decision requires no thought, than the merely imperfect agent whose transgression represents a surrender or a falling away. Yet once we have acknowledged that it is fair to blame people for bad acts that flow automatically from bad traits over which they lack control, we can hardly deny that it is fair to blame them for those bad traits themselves.

Thus, our standard blaming practices stand in considerable tension (if they are not flatly inconsistent) with F's claim that it is never fair to blame people for what they cannot help. This of course does not compel us to abandon F, since we could instead abandon our blaming practices. However, the availability of this option is no threat to my claim that anyone who thinks it fair to blame people for their bad acts should also think it fair to blame them for their bad traits. Furthermore, the proffered option — to adopt what is in effect an error theory of blame — is so drastic that we should not take it unless compelled to do so by weighty reasons. Thus, as long as no independent defense of F is forthcoming — and, as has been noted, none appears to be in the offing — it will remain F, and not our standard blaming practices, that ought to go.[12]

---

12. One way to argue that the conflict requires the rejection of our blaming practices is to maintain that F itself is part of our concept of blame, which is therefore incoherent.

IV

By rejecting F, we eliminate the final reason for accepting (1)'s claim that control is a necessary condition for blame; and by abandoning that necessary condition, we remove the main obstacle to accepting BFT. However, it is one thing to say that we lack good reason to reject BFT and quite another to say that we have good reason to accept it. Thus, the question that remains is whether there is any positive case for BFT.

The answer, I think, is that there is, and that its main elements are implicit in two points that have already been made. The first, which entered as part of my argument that our inability to blame agents for acts over which they lack control is explained not by (1) but by a necessary condition for blameworthiness which applies differently to acts and to traits, was that a person's bad traits stand in an intimate enough relation *to* him to reflect badly *on* him. Although my original aim in making this point was simply to undermine one version of the main anti-BFT argument, I now want to re-invoke it in the service of a more positive conclusion—to show not just that we can accept BFT, but that we should.

To see how the intimacy of the connection between a person and his bad traits supports the conclusion that we are justified in condemning him for them, we need only remind ourself of how difficult it would be to condemn a person's bad traits *without* also condemning him. As we saw, to have a morally bad trait is to be systematically unresponsive to a certain class of moral reasons. It is to be disposed both to see bad acts of the relevant type as live options and actually to perform such acts whenever they seem sufficiently advantageous or attractive. It is, as well, to have a variety of associated cognitive and affective dispositions—dispositions to

---

This seems to be the position that Bernard Williams takes in *Ethics and the Limits of Philosophy* (Cambridge, Mass.: Harvard University Press, 1985). Williams suggests that F is internal to the concept of blame when he speaks of the moral system of which blame is a part as imposing a pressure to "cut through character and psychological or social determination, and allocate blame and responsibility on the ultimately fair basis of the agent's own contribution, no more and no less" (194). He also says that "[i]t is an illusion to suppose that this demand can be met" and that "[t]o the extent that the institution of blame works coherently, it does so because it attempts less than morality would like it to do" (ibid.). Of the two claims that Williams here advances, I accept the second but reject the first: as far as I can see, he offers no argument for the view that F is part of the very concept of blame.

notice vulnerability and enjoy its exploitation if one is cruel, to discern opportunities for self-advancement and disregard the interests of others if one is selfish, and so on. Taken together, these vice-related dispositions are bound to place their stamp on much of what an agent thinks and does. They are also bound to have their roots in stable patterns of interaction among the desires, beliefs, and finer-grained dispositions that together make him the person he is. For both reasons, there is no clear difference between condemning a person's cruelty, manipulativeness, or unfairness, and simply condemning *him*. It is something of an exaggeration, but not much of one, to say that where a person's vices are concerned, it is not possible to hate the disposition to sin but love the sinner because the sinner is in good measure constituted by his dispositions to sin.

The second point to which I want to return is that even when a bad act does fall within an agent's control, its badness is often a near-inevitable result of one or more bad traits over which he lacks control. In section III above, I made this point as part of my argument that blaming people for their bad traits is not unfair. Here, however, I want to argue that it, too, can be recycled to provide BFT with positive support.

To see this, consider an act whose badness is a near-inevitable result of a bad trait that the agent cannot help having. Suppose, for example, that a given person is so self-absorbed that he does not even realize how hurtful his words are, or that someone is so dishonest that it does not even occur to him to tell the truth when it is to his advantage to lie. Such a person, we have seen, is every bit as blameworthy as someone who performs an equally cruel or dishonest act after struggling with, and then surrendering to, what he fully recognizes as a bad impulse. Thus, it is evidently possible to deserve blame for bad acts that stem not from self-conscious decisions to flout moral reasons, but rather from vice-induced lapses in moral clarity. In a case of this sort, what we condemn the agent for is still the badness of the act itself, but the act's badness in turn is a direct and automatic consequence of the badness of the agent's character. However, once we have acknowledged that an agent can deserve blame for an act whose badness is a direct and automatic consequence of a bad trait over which he lacks control, we are hardly in a position to deny that he can also deserve blame for the bad trait itself.

Here, then, are two distinct arguments for BFT. Although their starting points are quite different—the first argument stresses the intimate relation between a person and his bad traits, the second, the intimate relation between a person's bad traits and his bad acts—they both converge on the idea that the boundaries between a person, his traits, and his acts are too fluid to sustain a compartmentalized approach to blame. Thus, each in its own way supports the conclusion that when a bad person acts badly, our condemnation is quite properly directed at both his behavior *and* his character.

This is not to deny that blame must sometimes be more narrowly focused. A person deserves blame for his behavior but not his character if his acting badly can be traced to a confluence of traits and situational factors none of which is itself bad—if, for example, someone who is normally gentle lashes out because he is tired, preoccupied, and a bit paranoid. Conversely, a person deserves blame for his character but not his behavior if he is (say) dishonest but simply has no occasion to lie. But what most needs stressing is not that such cases sometimes arise, but that they so often do not. In many ordinary contexts, people act badly because they are bad; and when they do, we naturally and properly blame them both for what they do and for what they are.

V

Although we have so far dealt only with blame, that concept is seldom viewed as standing alone. Instead, it is widely believed that blameworthiness presupposes responsibility—that to deserve blame for something, a person must be responsible for it. It is also widely believed that blame is importantly linked to punishment.[13] However, if we accept the first of

---

13. One philosopher who seems to take blame and responsibility to be conceptually linked is Susan Wolf, who speaks of "the particular kind of blame that is associated with the philosophical question of responsibility" (*Freedom Within Reason* [New York: Oxford University Press, 1990], 40). Another is Ronald Milo, who writes in *Immorality* (Princeton, N.J.: Princeton University Press, 1984) that "[d]isagreement about whether anyone is ever really blameworthy stems . . . from disagreement about the conditions requisite for moral responsibility" (227). One who adds punishment to the mix is John Martin Fischer, who says in the introduction to *Moral Responsibility* that "a person is a morally responsible agent when he is an *appropriate candidate* for the reactive attitudes and for such activities as praise and blame and punishment and reward" (12, emphasis in original).

these linkages, then won't the version of BFT that I have labeled "more interesting" imply that people are responsible even for bad traits they cannot help having? And if we accept the second, won't we have to say that bad people deserve punishment even when they have done nothing wrong?

Because any version of BFT that had these implications would be a bit too interesting, it is important to stress that blame, responsibility, and punishment are not really this closely related. In saying this, I certainly do not mean that they are unrelated. I readily acknowledge that no one can deserve blame for any *act* unless he is responsible for it; and although the issues raised by punishment are murkier, I think as well that desert of punishment presupposes desert of blame. However, none of this will damage BFT unless responsibility and punishment are at least as broadly applicable as blame—unless they can plausibly be said to apply to all the same kinds of things that it does. If, instead, there is independent reason to suppose that no one can be responsible or deserve punishment for anything except an act or omission or its effects, but no comparable reason to say this about blame, then BFT will not imply either that people are responsible for their bad traits or that they deserve to be punished for them.

And, in fact, both responsibility and desert of punishment do seem to apply exclusively to acts. Where responsibility is concerned, the limitation is implicit in the concept itself. Under its standard interpretation, responsibility is a causal notion. To be responsible for an outcome, a person or thing must play some role in causing or failing to prevent that outcome. This is true whether the relevant notion of responsibility is merely causal, as it is when a design flaw is said to be responsible for the collapse of a bridge, or whether it is moral, as when an engineer's negligence is said to be responsible for the design flaw.

However, merely to possess a trait is not to play any causal role at all: a person's traits are conceptually separable both from what he has done to bring them into existence and from what he does as a result of having them. Thus, the easiest way to show that responsibility for traits is incoherent is simply to point out that where a person's merely possessing (as opposed to causing, failing to prevent, or manifesting) a trait is concerned, the basic necessary condition for responsibility is never met.

Even by itself, this observation would suffice to show that responsibility for traits is incoherent. However, there is also a further route to that conclusion—a route that runs through a further necessary condition that a person must satisfy in order to be *morally* responsible for something.

When a person is jostled and consequently knocks over a fragile vase, he is not morally responsible for its breaking despite his involvement in the causal sequence; and the explanation is clearly that that sequence does not operate through his intellect or will. To exhibit the right sort of causal involvement, the agent must attempt to influence the outcome for a reason. Thus, in the current context, the term "responsible" retains its root meaning of "answerable": to be morally responsible for something is precisely to be subject to a request for one's reasons for causing or not preventing it. However, merely having (as opposed to cultivating) a particular character trait is obviously not something one does for a reason; so on these grounds, too, it seems unintelligible to suppose that someone might be morally responsible merely for having a bad character.

Because it does not make sense to hold someone responsible for being the kind of person he is, we can safely accept BFT without being forced to accept the implausible view that people are responsible simply for having their bad traits. However, we cannot similarly dismiss the possibility that BFT might commit us to the view that people deserve to be punished for their bad traits; for desert of punishment, unlike responsibility, is not essentially a causal notion. Whatever else is true, we can indeed make sense of the idea that a person might deserve to be punished simply for being bad.

Nevertheless, it is one thing to say that such desert is intelligible and quite another to say either that it is defensible or that BFT commits us to it. Moreover, when we examine the most influential retributive theories, we find that neither conclusion is warranted; for instead of taking desert of blame to imply desert of punishment, each such theory bases its justification of punishment on one or another normative principle that applies exclusively to acts. Thus, of the classical retributivists, Kant viewed punishment as redressing an imbalance that was created by the criminal's act,[14] while Hegel saw it as an appropriate response to the will that

---

14. Immanuel Kant, *The Philosophy of Law*, part II, trans. W. Hastie, in *Philosophical Perspectives on Punishment*, ed. Gertrude Ezorsky (Albany: State University of New York Press, 1972), 104. For discussion of Kant's views about the relation between deserved punishment and character, see Thomas Hill, "Kant's Anti-Moralistic Strain," in his *Dignity and Practical Reason in Kant's Moral Theory* (Ithaca, N.Y.: Cornell University Press, 1992), 176–95.

the criminal expressed *through* his act.[15] Among contemporary retributivists, Robert Nozick views punishment as a way of reconnecting
agents to the values they have flouted by acting wrongly,[16] while Herbert
Morris sees it as imposing an extra burden to offset the extra benefit that
the criminal gained by acting illegally.[17] None of these retributive theories, and no other such theory of which I am aware, saddles the proponent of BFT with the view that anyone deserves punishment merely
for having a bad character.

BFT therefore does not commit us to holding either that people are
responsible for their bad traits or that they deserve to be punished for
those traits. By purging BFT of these unwanted implications, we significantly increase its plausibility. However, at the same time, we may
appear to diminish its impact; for blame may seem significant precisely
because of its affiliations with responsibility and punishment. Once
these notions are stripped away, how much of importance remains?

The answer is: almost everything; for far from drawing its own
significance from its associations with responsibility and punishment,
blame is, if anything, the source of much of their significance. When
philosophers ask whether people are free in a sense that implies that
they are responsible for their acts, what is mainly at stake is the propriety
of reacting to them *as* responsible agents. Moreover, although the standard list of reactions that presuppose responsibility includes both positive and negative elements—the list encompasses praise and reward as
well as blame and punishment—it is the negative entries that dominate
our thinking. For reasons that are not entirely clear, the impulse to
blame and punish seems far more urgent than the impulse to praise and
reward. Moreover, of the former more urgent impulses, the impulse to
punish (as opposed to the justification for punishing) is itself a natural
extension of the hostility and other negative feelings that are often
associated with blame. In the end, it is largely our preoccupation with

15. G. W. F. Hegel, *The Philosophy of Right*, trans. F. M. Knox (Oxford: Oxford
University Press, 1942), sec. 100, 70.

16. Robert Nozick, *Philosophical Explanations* (Cambridge, Mass.: Harvard University Press, 1981), 383–84.

17. Herbert Morris, "Persons and Punishment," in his *On Guilt and Innocence*
(Berkeley and Los Angeles: University of California Press, 1976), 31–88.

blame that lends interest to this family of concepts. Thus, even when it is stripped of all accretions, blame, and by extension BFT, is bound to remain meaningful and important.

Just *why* blame is so important is, of course, a further question. Because my main emphasis so far has been on the relation between character and blameworthiness, I have not yet asked what it is that a person deserves when he deserves to be blamed; and still less have I asked why his getting what he deserves should loom as large, both to us and to him, as it evidently does. These questions are, if anything, even more difficult than the ones we have already addressed, and it is now time to consider them.

FIVE

WHAT BLAME IS NOT

BLAME IS PERPLEXING BOTH AS IT PERTAINS TO THE PERSON DOING THE blaming and as it pertains to the person blamed. Concerning the person doing the blaming, the basic question is what blame is; concerning the person blamed, it is why his wrongdoing or bad character should render him deserving of whatever blame is. Of the philosophers who have tried to answer the first question, some view blame as moral criticism aimed at improving conduct, others as a belief that someone's misconduct has marred his moral record, and still others as a negative emotional reaction triggered *by* misconduct. However, in the current chapter, I will argue that none of this will do. By coming to see what is wrong with each standard approach, we will also come to see why we must think of blame in some new way.

I

Blame is often viewed as the opposite of praise, and praise is always overtly bestowed.[1] To praise a person is to express admiration of some

---

1. Praise directed at God in silent prayer is not a counterexample because what is hidden from humans is accessible to God. From His perspective, silent praise is overtly bestowed.

meritorious act he has performed or of some excellence or virtue he possesses. And, just so, it may be held that blame, too, is essentially overt—that to blame someone is to express disapproval of, or contempt for, some bad act he has performed or some flaw in his character. Because expressions of disapproval and contempt can have aversive effects, this approach allows us to see how blame can be socially useful. Taking their cue from this, some utilitarians have held that to blame someone is simply to express disapproval of his bad behavior or character in a way that is calculated to mitigate or improve it.

One utilitarian who notoriously holds this view is J. J. C. Smart. That Smart takes praise as his paradigm, and that he views blame as simply its negative counterpart, is evident from the following passage:

> Praising a person is...an important act in itself—it has significant effects. A utilitarian must therefore learn to control his acts of praise and dispraise, thus perhaps concealing his approval of an action when he thinks that the expression of such approval might have bad effects, and perhaps even praising actions of which he does not really approve.[2]

Along similar lines, though with an emphasis on the blame that we direct at people for their bad traits rather than their bad acts, another utilitarian, P. H. Nowell-Smith, has written that

> [the theory that vices are traits whose effects are typically bad] enables us to understand why it is not only moral weakness that is blamed, but also wickedness....A wicked character can be improved by moral censure and punishment; and if we really thought that a man was so bad as to be irremediable we should, I think, cease to blame him, though we might impose restraints on him as we would on a mad dog.[3]

Although neither author is explicit about the mechanism through which blame (or "dispraise") affects action or character, I take their point to be that it works by eliciting shame, remorse, fear, or some other feeling that

2. J. J. C. Smart, "An Outline of a System of Utilitarian Ethics," in J. J. C. Smart and Bernard Williams, *Utilitarianism: For and Against* (Cambridge: Cambridge University Press, 1973), 49–50.

3. P. H. Nowell-Smith, *Ethics* (Baltimore, Md.: Penguin Books, 1954), 306.

the wrongdoer finds unpleasant and hence will subsequently seek to avoid. While unpleasant feelings are generally less burdensome than fines, imprisonment, or execution, any activity that associates them with wrongdoing is indeed likely to have some deterrent effect. Hence, if we accept the utilitarian account, we will in effect treat blame as punishment light.[4]

There is, however, wide agreement that we should not accept that account. As one of its few recent defenders, Richard Arneson, has noted with relish, it is "the position everyone loves to hate."[5] Among the standard reasons for rejecting it are, first, that the utility of expressing disapproval "depends on too many factors other than the nature of the act in question"[6] to coincide with our intuitions about when agents are blameworthy, and, second, that even if expressing disapproval did increase utility in just those cases in which agents intuitively seem blameworthy, this would remain an accident: the account would still "[do] nothing like justice to the real nature of our praise- and blame-related responses."[7] Given the evident force of these objections, we must indeed reject the utilitarian justification of blame.

However, even if we do, it does not follow that we must also reject the associated account of what blame *is*. It is entirely consistent to say, first, that whether someone deserves to be blamed depends not on the utility of blaming him but rather on the moral quality of what he has done or is, but also, second, that what a blameworthy person deserves is just what Smart and Nowell-Smith took blame to be—namely, an

4. Views of this sort are advanced in Moritz Schlick, " When Is a Man Responsible?" in *Free Will and Determinism*, ed. Bernard Berofsky (New York: Harper and Row, 1966), 54–63, and J. J. C. Smart, "Free Will, Praise, and Blame," in *Determinism, Free Will, and Moral Responsibility*, ed. Gerald Dworkin (Englewood Cliffs, N.J.: Prentice-Hall, 1970), 196–213.

5. Richard Arneson, "The Smart Theory of Moral Responsibility and Desert," in *Desert and Justice*, ed. Serena Olsaretti (Oxford: Oxford University Press, 2003), 233.

6. T. M. Scanlon, "The Significance of Choice," in *Equal Freedom: Selected Tanner Lectures on Human Values*, ed. Stephen Darwall (Ann Arbor: University of Michigan Press, 1995), 48.

7. Jonathan Bennett, "Accountability," in *Philosophical Subjects: Essays Presented to P. F. Strawson*, ed. Zak Van Straaten (Oxford: Oxford University Press, 1980), 20.

expression of our disapproval of what he has done or is. Thus, considered simply as a view about the nature of blame, their position remains untouched by the standard criticisms.

It is, however, clearly deficient on other grounds, the most obvious of which is that we can blame a person without his even being aware of it. Far from always being public, as deterrent punishment necessarily is, the blame that we direct at wrongdoers can be kept entirely private. As Richard Brandt once noted, "a cool handshake, a reproachful glance, would ordinarily be described rather as symptoms of blaming than as cases of it."[8] This does not mean that blaming someone cannot affect his behavior, but it does mean that the blame itself must be distinct from any utterance or action through which it is expressed. To blame someone is one thing, to communicate one's blame, another.[9]

Even by itself, this objection seems decisive. However, there is also a more subtle difficulty with the view that blaming is simply expressing disapproval with the aim of affecting future conduct. Put most briefly, the further difficulty is that even when someone does express disapproval of another's conduct or character, the way his words influence the other's behavior is precisely by causing him to believe that the speaker actually has the attitude they express. If instead the other believes this attitude is absent—if he thinks the speaker does not really blame him, but is only acting as though he does—then the speaker's words are unlikely to have the desired effect. Unlike the standard forms of punishment, which owe their deterrent value to the fact that they are unpleasant in themselves, expressions of disapproval are unpleasant only because of the attitude they convey. This reinforces our previous conclusion that if we wish to understand blame, it is not these expressions, but rather the attitude they express, upon which we must focus.

8. Richard Brandt, "Blameworthiness and Obligation," in *Essays in Moral Philosophy*, ed. A. I. Melden (Seattle: University of Washington Press, 1958), 8.

9. Compare R. Jay Wallace: "Though blame often and naturally finds expression in sanctioning behavior, it is not necessarily so expressed—thus I can blame a person 'privately' without expressing my response to anyone at all, much less sanctioning the person whom I blame (who may anyway be outside my sphere of causal influence)" (R. Jay Wallace, *Responsibility and the Moral Sentiments* [Cambridge, Mass.: Harvard University Press, 1994], 56).

II

But what kind of attitude might this be? Because we cannot blame someone unless we believe various things about him, and because our beliefs are among the attitudes we can keep to ourselves, one obvious possibility is that blame just is a belief or combination of beliefs. However, this suggestion becomes problematic as soon as we ask which combination of beliefs might add up to blame.

For, first, we obviously cannot equate blaming someone exclusively with believing that he has acted badly. This proposal is hopeless because the question we are trying to answer is precisely what blaming someone adds to believing that he has acted badly. Far from expressing any belief that is equivalent to blaming, "explain[ing] to the offender that what he did was wrong" was Pereboom's central example of what would remain possible if we were to abandon blame. Nor, just as obviously, can we say that what blaming someone adds to believing that he has acted badly is the further belief that his wrongdoing renders him blame*worthy*; for this merely returns us to the question of what, in blaming the wrongdoer, we believe him to be worthy of. Thus, the central challenge to the view that blame is simply a combination of beliefs is to specify exactly what the blamer is supposed to believe.

Interestingly, those who take up the challenge invariably express their answer in metaphorical terms. One common metaphor is that of a blemish or stain; while Smart obviously does not accept the view, he snidely suggests that someone who blames another "may be saying that there is something like a yellow stain on the other man's soul."[10] Alternatively and less vividly, the guiding metaphor may involve records and bookkeeping, as when Jonathan Glover writes that "[i]nvolved in our present practice of blaming is a kind of moral accounting, where a person's actions are recorded in an informal balance sheet, with the object of assessing his moral worth."[11] Combining variants of both metaphors, Michael Zimmerman summarizes the blame-as-belief proposal this way:

---

10. Smart, "Outline of a System of Utilitarian Ethics," 52.
11. Jonathan Glover, *Responsibility* (London: Routledge and Kegan Paul, 1970), 64.

> Praising someone may be said to constitute judging that there is a "credit" in his "ledger of life," or a "positive mark" in his "report-card of life," or a "luster" on his "record as a person"; that his "record" has been "burnished"; that his "moral standing" has been "enhanced." Blaming someone may be said to constitute judging that there is a "discredit" or "debit" in his "ledger," or a "negative mark" in his "report card," or a "blemish" or "stain" on his "record"; that his "record" has been "tarnished"; that his "moral standing" has been "diminished."[12]

Should we agree that to blame someone is just to have a belief of one of these sorts?

If this question turned on either the intelligibility or the truth of what the blamer is said to believe, its answer would almost certainly be "no." There is no evidence either that we have souls or that if we had them they would be the kinds of things that could be marred by our misdeeds; and neither is it clear in what sense a person's performing a very good deed can offset or cancel his performing a very bad one, or who if anyone is keeping score. Because we lack answers to such questions, it is tempting to dismiss the view that each bad act stains the agent's soul or reduces his moral balance as a calcified remnant of a now largely discarded religious morality. Yet even if we do dismiss that view, it does not follow that we must also dismiss the view that what blaming someone adds to believing that he has acted badly is simply a *belief* that his bad act has reduced his moral balance or stained his soul; for even falsehoods can be widely believed and even incoherencies embraced *as* beliefs.

There are, however, plenty of other reasons to reject that view. One early sign of trouble is that blame and acceptance of the relevant propositions are far from coextensive. Many who are quite willing to blame wrongdoers would explicitly disavow both the suggestion that each of us is soiled by his past misdeeds and the suggestion that we are all perpetually running a moral tab. A further problem with the latter suggestion is that it carries the implausible implication that it is impossible to blame someone without making implicit reference to his whole moral history. However, instead of pursuing either difficulty, I

---

12. Michael Zimmerman, *An Essay on Moral Responsibility* (Totowa, N.J.: Rowman and Littlefield, 1988), 38.

want to proceed directly to what I view as the central objection to the belief account—namely, that it utterly fails to capture the role that blame actually plays in our emotional lives.

That blame plays some significant emotional role can hardly be denied. This is evident from the energy we expend in trying to affix it, from the rancor that often accompanies it, and from the urgency with which we seek to avoid it. Whatever their errors, those who view blame exclusively as a mechanism of social control are clearly right to hold that being blamed is often unpleasant enough to have a deterrent effect. Thus, if the view that blame is a belief about a person's moral balance or the state of his soul is to be at all tenable, its proponents must somehow explain why this is so.

But what, exactly, might the explanation be? Why, if what blaming someone adds to believing that he has acted badly is simply the further belief that his bad act has reduced his moral balance or stained his soul, should we be any more bothered by the knowledge that others blame us than by the knowledge that they believe we have acted badly? Why should we care whether they also believe that our bad action has reduced our moral balance or stained our soul? Indeed, if anything aside from our bad action and the fact that others are aware of it bothers us, shouldn't it be simply the further fact that the bad action *has* reduced our moral balance or stained our soul—a fact that, if it obtains at all, is one that would obtain whether or not anyone else believed that it did? And, hence, shouldn't the further belief that is said to constitute the blame be one to which we are completely indifferent?[13]

To this objection, there may seem to be an obvious reply. Even if we do not care whether others believe that our bad action has reduced

---

13. One possible reason not to want others to believe that one's moral balance is low or negative is that someone who believed this would in effect believe that one is a bad person. However, the desire not be viewed as a bad person will at best explain why we do not want others to believe that our moral balance has been reduced *when we expect them to infer that that reduction brings our moral balance below some crucial threshold.* This proposal therefore does not explain why we dislike being blamed even by persons who will not infer this—for example, by persons who do not know our moral history or who believe that our past behavior was so good (or so bad) that our current balance is far from the crucial threshold. *Mutatis mutandis,* the same can be said about the claim that the desire not to be thought a bad person provides us with a reason not to want others to believe that our souls are stained.

our moral balance or stained our soul, we obviously do dislike it when others are angry or hostile toward us. Moreover, it is undeniable that people often are angry or hostile toward those whom they blame. Thus, simply by appropriating the rancor that often accompanies blame, can't those who equate blame with a belief that someone's bad action has reduced his moral balance or stained his soul provide a natural explanation of why we all dislike being blamed?

The answer, I think, is that they can, but that in so doing, they merely shift the problem to another place. Instead of having to explain why anyone cares whether others believe that his bad action has stained his soul or reduced his moral balance, they now have to explain why those who believe that someone's bad action has stained his soul or reduced his moral balance should be hostile or angry toward him. At least offhand, the far more natural reactions to the thought that some-one has inflicted this sort of harm upon himself are pity on the one hand and satisfaction on the other; while the far more likely cause of any associated anger or hostility is the simpler belief that he has acted badly. However, if it is this simpler belief that evokes the anger, then the belief that the current proposal takes to be essential to blame—the belief that the wrongdoer's transgression has stained his soul or reduced his moral balance—will drop out as irrelevant. For this reason, the proposed ac-count will shed no light on why we dislike being blamed (as opposed to being thought to have acted badly) as much as we do.

And neither, finally, does that account shed any light on our per-vasive preoccupation with affixing blame. It is easy enough to see why we might want to know whether what someone did on a given occasion was bad, but much harder to see why we should take any interest in either his moral balance or the state of his soul. It is, however, an interest of one of these sorts that would have to motivate our efforts to acquire the beliefs of which the current proposal takes blame to consist. Thus, if we accept that proposal, we will have to concede that the powerful human urge to blame wrongdoers remains a mystery.

III

I have just argued that the penumbra of emotion that surrounds blame is far more likely to attach to the belief that the person blamed has acted badly than to any further belief about the impact of the bad action on his moral balance sheet or soul. This argument, if sound, will tell heavily against the blame-as-belief account; but it may also point the way to something better. The alternative to which it points is that the anger and hostility that accompany blame are not merely the effects of whatever blaming someone adds to believing that he has acted badly, but are precisely the additional element itself. On this alternative view, to blame someone just is to have a negative emotional reaction to him because we believe that he has acted badly or is a bad person.

This proposal, that what blaming someone adds to believing that he has acted badly is some sort of negative emotional reaction to him, preserves the advantages of each previous proposal while avoiding its defects. Like the utilitarian attempt to assimilate blame to punishment but unlike the blame-as-belief view, the current proposal allows us to acknowledge that—and to explain why—blame often functions as an instrument of social control; while like the blame-as-belief view but unlike the utilitarian account, it also allows us to acknowledge blame's essentially private nature. Perhaps because it offers this combination of advantages, the view that blame essentially involves some negative affective element is very widely accepted.

Its most influential statement is again Strawson's landmark essay "Freedom and Resentment." Speaking of the blame-related attitudes of indignation and disapprobation, Strawson wrote that these attitudes

> like resentment, tend to inhibit or at least to limit our goodwill towards [their] objects..., tend to promote an at least partial and temporary withdrawal of goodwill; they do so in proportion as they are strong; and their strength is in general proportioned to what is felt to be the magnitude of the injury and to the degree to which the agent's will is identified with, or indifferent to, it. (These, of course, are not contingent connections.)[14]

Our partial withdrawal of good will, Strawson added, involves a "modification...of the general demand that another should, if possible, be spared suffering."[15]

14. Strawson, "Freedom and Resentment," 138.
15. Ibid.

In the forty-odd years since the publication of Strawson's essay, many others have adopted variants of this position. One contemporary philosopher, Gary Watson, has recently written that

> in a Strawsonian view, blaming is not merely a fault-finding appraisal—which could be made from a detached and austerely "objective" standpoint—but a range of responses to the agent on the basis of such appraisals. These nonpropositional responses...make up a wide spectrum. Negative reactive attitudes range from bombing Tripoli to thinking poorly of a person.[16]

Another contemporary, R. Jay Wallace, asserts that "to blame a person is to be subject to one of [the] reactive emotions because of what the person has done."[17] And Roger Wertheimer puts the same point more flamboyantly when he writes that condemnation "[l]ike punishment...is assaultive, expressing aggressive antipathy, anger, hatred, or disgust"[18] and that those who condemn "favor some suffering for the condemned."[19]

Although these philosophers have modified both Strawson's account of what we blame people for and his characterization of what blame consists of—Strawson describes both in terms of a lack of good will while his followers hold instead that what we blame people for are moral transgressions and that blame itself is a negative feeling such as hostility or anger—their proposals remain true to his basic insight that blame is fundamentally an affective phenomenon.

Should we agree that a measure of hostility, or a partial withdrawal of good will, is what blaming someone adds to merely believing that he has acted badly? Despite its current popularity, I think this proposal is deeply problematic for a number of reasons, the most important of which is that it prevents us from making sense of the idea that blame is something of which a wrongdoer can be worthy or that he can deserve.

---

16. Gary Watson, "Responsibility and the Limits of Evil," in *Responsibility, Character, and the Emotions: New Essays in Moral Psychology*, ed. Ferdinand Schoeman (Cambridge: Cambridge University Press, 1987), 262.

17. Wallace, *Responsibility and the Moral Sentiments*, 75.

18. Roger Wertheimer, "Constraining Condemning," *Ethics* 108 (April 1998): 493.

19. Wertheimer, "Constraining Condemning," 491.

Because the issues here are complex, I shall develop my objection in several stages: first, by arguing that the uncompromising naturalism that leads Strawson to propose his account of blame is in deep tension with the idea that anyone can be blameworthy; second, by arguing that even if we reject Strawson's broader commitments, we will still have trouble integrating the affective account with our central beliefs about blameworthiness; and, finally, by introducing a number of counter-examples to the affective account itself.

IV

Most contemporary philosophers who accept versions of Strawson's account of blame are quite willing to use the language of blameworthiness. They are quite willing to combine the claim that blame essentially involves some sort of negative affective response to a wrongdoer with the further claim that blame as so construed can be deserved. By contrast, Strawson's own argument commits him to denying that anyone is blameworthy at a deep level. To see why, we must briefly review the reasoning that led him to formulate his account.

Strawson's topic in "Freedom and Resentment" was the free will debate, and in particular the disagreement between the "pessimists" (hard determinists) who believe that responsibility requires an unattainable contracausal freedom and the "optimists" (compatibilists) who believe that persons are responsible whenever their behavior is susceptible to manipulation by reward and punishment. Because Strawson viewed both alternatives as unsatisfactory, he sought to provide an account of responsibility that avoids both the "panicky metaphysics of libertarianism" and the facile instrumentalism of many compatibilists. To accomplish that aim, he rejected the assumption—shared by both camps—that responsibility, if it exists, is a feature of persons that is presupposed by, and legitimizes, such reactive attitudes as blame. Reversing the usual ordering, Strawson urged that we understand responsibility in terms of our susceptibility to the reactive attitudes themselves. He argued, first, that our tendency to withdraw good will from persons whose own behavior displays a lack of it is a primitive fact about us, and, second, that to be responsible for one's acts is precisely to be someone whose failures to display good will are in fact prone to elicit such responses. What distinguishes the blame-related reactive attitudes from others is only that the blame-related attitudes are "vicarious": they are, or might be, responses to behavior that displays a lack of good will toward persons other than the respondent himself.

There is, as a matter of logic, no incompatibility between Strawson's claim that blame, construed as involving a withdrawal of good will, is a natural human response, and the further claim that those whose behavior reflects a lack of good will deserve to be blamed. These claims would both be true if those who react to a lack of good will in others by withdrawing their own were thereby manifesting a natural disposition to recognize and respond to the blameworthiness of the ill-willed. However, given Strawson's view that responsibility is not an independent feature of persons, he is unlikely to view blameworthiness as an independent feature of persons either. To do so would be to reintroduce, in only slightly altered guise, the fruitless dispute between the pessimist and the optimist.

The suggestion that Strawson is unlikely to view blameworthiness as an independent feature of persons, and *a fortiori* is unlikely to view blame as a response to any such feature, is borne out by various things he says. That the blame we direct at wrongdoers is not justified by their blameworthiness appears to be an implication of his contention that

> inside the general structure or web of human attitudes and feelings of which I have been speaking, there is endless room for modification, redirection, criticism, and justification. But questions of justification are internal to the structure or related to modifications internal to it. The existence of the general framework of attitudes themselves is something we are given with the fact of human society. As a whole, it neither calls for, nor permits, an external "rational" justification.[20]

Strawson also appears to disavow the suggestion that blame can be grounded in desert when he memorably characterizes the "intuition of fittingness" as "a pitiful intellectualist trinket for a philosopher to wear against the recognition of his own humanity."[21] Perhaps taking his cue

---

20. Strawson, "Freedom and Resentment," 140.
21. Ibid.

from these assertions, Jonathan Bennett reads Strawson as maintaining that

> my feeling of indignation at what you have done is not a perception of your objective blameworthiness, nor is it demanded of me by such a perception. It expresses my emotional make-up, rather than reflecting my ability to recognize a blame-meriting person when I see one.[22]

As should be apparent, I think Bennett's reading of Strawson is exactly right. However, I also think that before we can accept Bennett's reading, we must consider one aspect of Strawson's discussion that may seem to tell against it. The difficulty I have in mind is that Strawson devotes considerable attention to the sorts of excuses that are commonly taken to render blame inappropriate. This aspect of his discussion seems significant because his acknowledgement that various excuses render blame unreasonable may appear to commit him to the view that blame is reasonable— that is, deserved—whenever someone acts badly without an excuse.[23]

I think, in fact, that Strawson's treatment of excuses does not commit him to any interesting version of this view; but before I can explain why, I must briefly summarize what he says. According to Strawson, there are two main types of circumstance in which the negative reactive attitudes, including the blame-related vicarious reactions of indignation and condemnation, are inappropriate. They are inappropriate, first, when an agent either acts in ignorance of the harm he is causing or else causes that harm under some kind of compulsion, and, second, when an agent is either "not himself" due to some kind of abnormal influence or stress

22. Bennett, "Accountability," 24.

23. Another apparent piece of evidence that Strawson does not wish to deny that wrongdoers can be blameworthy is his assertion that "[b]y attending to that complicated web of attitudes and feelings which form an essential part of the moral life as we know it . . . [we can] recover from the facts as we know them a sense of what we mean, i.e., of *all* we mean, when, speaking the language of morals, we speak of desert" (Strawson, "Freedom and Resentment," 139; emphasis in original). However, what I take Strawson to mean here is only that we can make distinctions between those who are deserving and those who are not *within* "the general structure or web of human attitudes and feelings" that neither requires not permits an external justification.

or—the more important possibility—is disqualified by the fact that he is "warped or deranged, abnormal or just a child."[24] In cases of the first type, the excusing condition is said to render blame inappropriate by showing that we cannot reasonably take the agent to have failed to manifest good will—that "the fact of injury was not in this case incompatible with that demand's having been met."[25] In cases of the second type, blame is said to be inappropriate for the more fundamental reason that we are justified in viewing the agent "as *incapacitated* in some or all respects for ordinary inter-personal relations,"[26] and thus as not a proper object for a demand that he display good will.

Bearing in mind these explanations of why excuses render blame unreasonable, let us return to the suggestion that Strawson's acknowledgement that excuses render blame unreasonable commits him to holding that blame can be reasonable when an agent lacks an excuse. This suggestion, we can now see, rests on a non sequitur; for what Strawson takes the absence of an excuse to render unreasonable is not the withdrawal of good will of which blame is said to consist, but only the beliefs that are said to trigger that withdrawal. What an agent's not having an excuse for an act that harms another gives us reason to believe about him is, first, that his harmful act really did manifest a lack of good will, and, second, that when he performed the act, he was not incapable of manifesting good will. These are precisely the facts about a person that Strawson takes to cause us to withdraw our good will from him. However, from the fact that someone has reason to hold a belief that *causes* him to withdraw good will from another, it simply does not follow that he also has reason *to* withdraw good will from the other. For this reason, Strawson's treatment of excuses implies only that the beliefs to which blame is a response admit of justification, but not that blame itself admits of justification. And because his treatment of excuses does not imply that blame itself is ever justified, it also does not imply that anyone is blameworthy in any sense that might *provide* the justification for blaming him.[27]

24. Strawson, "Freedom and Resentment," 126.

25. Ibid., 125.

26. Ibid., 129.

27. Because Strawson takes our blaming someone to be contingent on our holding beliefs about him that can be either reasonable or unreasonable, his position makes it

V

Given his general philosophical commitments, Strawson is hardly in a position to treat a wrongdoer's desert of blame—or, *a fortiori*, his desert of the withdrawal of good will of which blame is said to consist—as a fact about him that antedates or justifies any actual withdrawal of good will. However, it is one thing to say that Strawson himself is not in a position to accept this combination of views, and quite another to say that *no one* can accept it. Thus, the obvious next question is whether someone who is less relentlessly naturalistic than Strawson himself can plausibly combine the view that blame essentially involves anger or the withdrawal of good will with the view that blame as so construed can be deserved.

The answer, I think, is that these views cannot plausibly be combined—that instead of sliding smoothly into the groove that blame-worthiness creates for blame, the affective account sticks and catches at places that betray its naturalistic origins. To see that the elements of the combined account are fundamentally mismatched, we need only look more closely at what that account would have to involve.

We can, if we like, conceal any anger or lack of good will that we harbor toward a wrongdoer. Thus, if it is true both that anger or a lack of good will is what blaming someone adds to believing that he has acted badly and that blame as so construed can be deserved, then it must also be

---

possible to define "blameworthy" exclusively in terms of the reasonableness of the relevant beliefs. A Strawsonian could say, if he liked, that when a person lacks an excuse for inflicting injury on another, that person is blameworthy precisely in the sense that it is reasonable to believe both that his action manifests a lack of good will and that he is not incapable of manifesting good will. However, when attributions of blameworthiness are understood in this way, they carry no implication that we may reasonably withdraw our own good will from the agent; and so neither, when combined with Strawson's view that a withdrawal of good will is an essential component of blame, do they imply that we may reasonably blame the agent. This makes it clear that the proposed definition is purely stipulative; for to call someone blameworthy in the standard sense is precisely to imply that we do have reason to blame him. Thus, as long as "blameworthy" is understood in its ordinary sense, Bennett's claim that Strawson accepts the view that no one is objectively blameworthy will remain fully consistent with what Strawson says about excuses.

true that wrongdoers can receive all the blame they deserve without ever knowing it. Even when someone receives his full measure of deserved blame, his receiving it need not affect his life at all. This implication is noteworthy because in many other contexts a person's getting what he deserves necessarily does have some impact on his life. However, what the implication shows is not that the combined account is unacceptable, but only that in order to accept it, we must take "X deserves blame" to mean no more than that blame directed at X is justified or appropriate—an interpretation that is in any case forced upon us by our earlier observation that *blame itself* can be kept strictly private.

Because the normative element of the combined account must thus be oriented to the person doing the blaming rather than the person blamed—because the account must view deserved blame not as something a wrongdoer "has coming to him" but rather as a response that his transgression renders appropriate in others—the account raises questions both about which others may appropriately have the response and about how long they may appropriately have it. Although each question can be answered in various ways, there is, in each case, good reason to opt for inclusiveness.

For, first, if we are to capture the detached, impartial quality that Strawson rightly takes to distinguish blame from resentment, we can hardly restrict those in whom anger or a lack of good will toward a wrongdoer is appropriate to persons who are themselves affected by his transgression. There is, moreover, no non-arbitrary basis for excluding any persons who are not affected. For this reason, the combined view is best taken to assert that *anyone* who knows what a wrongdoer has done—including the wrongdoer himself—may appropriately react to him with anger or a withdrawal of good will. And, along similar lines, to capture the important idea that a wrongdoer can deserve blame now for something he did a long time ago, the combined view is best taken to assert that those reactions remain appropriate long after the transgression itself.

When both clarifications are made explicit, they yield a version of the combined account which equates the claim that an agent is blameworthy with the claim that anyone who knows that the agent has acted badly within some unspecified but substantial stretch of the past may appropriately react to him with anger or a lack of good will. However, when the view is seen to have this underlying structure, it can also be seen to be vulnerable to at least three serious objections.

The first objection is that its implications are far too dark to be credible. Because we all sometimes act wrongly in ways that are readily apparent, it is not unreasonable to suppose that virtually everyone is known by each of his acquaintances to have recently performed at least one blameworthy act. This supposition, when conjoined with the combined view's claim that any recent blameworthy act renders it appropriate for anyone who knows about it to be angry at, or to lack good will toward, the agent, supports the conclusion that it is appropriate for everyone to be angry at, or to lack good will toward, virtually everyone else he knows. That conclusion, however, is in effect a *reductio*; for whatever else is true, perpetual mutual hostility is hardly an appropriate ideal of human interaction.

Because I have offered no interpretation of "appropriate," it is possible (though I think unlikely) that someone might avoid this objection by adopting a very weak version of that notion. However, any progress that was made along these lines would only worsen the second objection, which is precisely that the proposed account of what it is to be blameworthy is *too* weak to do justice to the importance of blameworthiness within our moral scheme. The difficulty here is that anger and the withdrawal of good will are hardly the only appropriate reactions to bad acts: we may just as appropriately react by being saddened, turning the other cheek, turning away, becoming disillusioned, trying to change society, trying to reason with the wrongdoer, or in any number of other ways. The fact that these reactions seem no less appropriate than anger does not mean that it is wrong either to explicate blame in terms of anger or to explicate blameworthiness in terms of the appropriateness of blame; but it does mean that blameworthiness as so explicated will enjoy no particular priority over sadnessworthiness, turning-the-other-cheekworthiness, or any other kind of reactionworthiness.

It is widely acknowledged that judging acts to be wrong is different from judging agents to be blameworthy; and it is widely acknowledged, too, that both sorts of evaluation are morally fundamental. To capture the fact that blameworthiness is a fundamental evaluative category, we must, at a minimum, construe being blameworthy as having some kind of negative moral status. However, according to the combined account, to call a wrongdoer blameworthy is not to say anything about his moral status, but is if anything to say something about the moral status of those who react to him with anger or a withdrawal of good will. Thus, the third and final objection to the combined account is that the structural feature to which I called attention at the outset—that the account is oriented to the person doing the blaming rather than the person blamed—renders mysterious our sense that to call someone blameworthy is to pass a negative moral judgment on *him*.

VI

For all the reasons cited, we cannot plausibly combine Strawson's affective account of blame with the idea that blame can be deserved. Given the importance that we attach to judgments of blameworthiness, I take this incompatibility to tell strongly against the affective account. However, if the case for the affective account were strong enough, its incompatibility with blameworthiness could also be taken to show that we should abandon the latter notion. Because this possibility remains open, it is important to realize that the affective account is also unacceptable on independent grounds.

The basic difficulty with that account is that the generalization upon which it rests—that blame is always accompanied by hostility or a withdrawal of good will—is far from airtight. Although this generalization is obviously instanced in many cases—it clearly holds, for example, when we shout at a driver whom we blame for thoughtlessly cutting us off, react with contempt to a swindler whom we blame for taking advantage of the vulnerable, or excoriate a friend whom we blame for betraying our secrets—it seems to fail in many others. We may, for example, feel no hostility toward the loved one whom we blame for failing to tell a sensitive acquaintance a hard truth, the criminal whom we blame for a burglary we read about in the newspaper, or the historical figure whom we blame for the misdeeds he performed long ago. As the latter examples suggest, blaming is something that we can do regretfully or dispassionately and that need not be accompanied by any rancor or withdrawal of good will. At least offhand, it seems perfectly consistent to suppose, first, that the stance I take toward my daughter for shading the truth about how much of her homework she has done is genuine blame, but, second, that that stance involves no modification at all "of the general demand that another should, if possible, be spared suffering."

If there can be affectless blame, then what blaming someone adds to believing that he has acted badly cannot be a negative affective response.

However, not all negative affective responses are dramatic; some involve only a twinge of irritation or a hint of malice. Taking his cue from this, Roger Wertheimer has remarked that "[c]ondemnation isn't defined by liters of blood lusted for. A condemner may hanker for the slightest of suffering: a quick squirm under a mild scold may suffice."[28] Wertheimer's remarks are relevant because a flicker of irritation is much easier to overlook than (say) a massive surge of rage. This opens up the possibility that a proponent of the affective account might try to block the objection that there can be affectless blame by insisting that we do always have negative feelings when we blame someone, but that those feelings are sometimes so faint that we simply don't notice them.

I must confess that even when I pay close attention, I don't always detect the flicker of annoyance or the muted desire to inflict suffering that this rejoinder says I must feel whenever I blame my daughter. However, even if I am deceiving myself here—the reader is invited to check his own reactions—the rejoinder will remain unconvincing in other contexts. The fundamental problem is not that it fails when the person blamed is someone we love or like or with whom we are otherwise involved, but rather that it at best *succeeds* in cases of this sort. The faintness of our emotions cannot plausibly be said to account for our apparent lack of rancor when we blame anonymous strangers—persons whom we have never met and who may be geographically or temporally remote—because we blame far too many such people to be able to feel anything about all of them. We simply do not have the emotional resources to muster even a twinge of hostility toward each of the innumerable miscreants, scoundrels, and thugs—many of them long dead—whom we blame for what we know to be their bad behavior or bad character. Hence, at least in cases of this less personal sort, the reaction I have characterized as affectless blame really does seem affectless.

But is it also really blame? At least according to R. Jay Wallace, it is not. Wallace candidly acknowledges that

> you may believe that an especially charming colleague who has cheated and lied to you has done something morally wrong, insofar

---

28. Wertheimer, "Constraining Condemning," 493.

as he has violated a moral obligation not to cheat or lie for personal advantage, and yet you may have trouble working up any resentment or indignation about his case.[29]

However, as Wallace sees it, such cases pose no threat to the Strawsonian account because our attitude toward someone like the charming colleague is not blame itself but only a closely related belief. What we believe, Wallace says, is only that the colleague is worthy of blame:

[o]n the reactive account, blame requires that you actually are subject to a reactive emotion, but an emotional response of this sort is not necessarily required for you to hold your colleague morally blameworthy.[30]

To hold the colleague blameworthy is in turn to believe that feelings of anger or hostility toward him would be appropriate if one were to have them; it is to believe that

such emotions would be warranted on our part, despite the fact that we happen not to feel them, and that they would be warranted in virtue of the fact that a moral obligation we accept has been violated.[31]

I think, in fact, that it is inaccurate to describe our attitude toward the charming colleague as anything other than blame itself. However, this claim is apt to be controversial, and in any case is relevant only to the meaning of "blame" and not to the nature of the phenomenon it designates. For both reasons, I will not challenge the linguistic propriety of Wallace's proposal, but will instead end by calling attention to two further problems that it raises.

The first, predictably, is that Wallace's reconstruction of what it is to hold someone blameworthy comes perilously close to committing him to the combined account against which I argued above. I say only that Wallace comes perilously close to accepting the combined

29. Wallace, *Responsibility and the Moral Sentiments*, 76.

30. Ibid., 76–77.

31. Ibid., 77.

account, but not quite that he does accept it, because there may (just) be room for him to say that what you believe when you hold your colleague blameworthy—namely, that feelings of anger or hostility would be appropriate if you were to have them—is in fact false. However, it is far from clear that Wallace *wants* to say this—his doing so would seem to contradict his own assertion that "the reactive emotions are made appropriate by certain kinds of beliefs, about the violation of the moral obligations we hold people to"[32]—and neither is it clear that saying it would allow him to avoid accepting the combined account's claim that "X is blameworthy" *means* that a hostile response to X would be appropriate.

The other problem with Wallace's way of dealing with the problem of affectless blame is that we can easily imagine variants of our original cases in which the subject not only feels no anger toward the wrongdoer whom he blames, but also holds some belief which implies that his feeling such anger would be positively inappropriate. To cite just three of the many possibilities, the subject might view it as emotionally extravagant to allow himself to be bothered by each of the countless individuals whom he blames for violating moral norms; might believe it is pointless to remain angry at a dead person whom he still blames for a past misdeed; or might consider it unloving to want his errant daughter to undergo any suffering at all. Because each belief implies that anger would be an inappropriate response to the person blamed, each seems flatly inconsistent with the belief that anger at him would be appropriate. Thus, just as we can find counterexamples to the claim that blame always involves a negative emotional response to the person blamed, so too can we find counterexamples to the claim that every instance of affectless blame is one in which the blamer at least believes that a negative emotional response to the person blamed would be appropriate.

32. Ibid.

SIX

WHAT BLAME IS

IN THE PREVIOUS CHAPTER, I ARGUED THAT THE STANDARD THEORIES OF blame are all inadequate—that blame is too private to be a public performance, too closely linked to motivation and affect to be a mere set of beliefs, and too compatible with both cold detachment and warm affection to be even partly constituted by anger. Given the inadequacy of these proposals, our guiding question—what does blame add to the belief that someone has acted badly or is a bad person?—has evidently not been answered. However, although the standard theories do not themselves identify the missing element, the phenomena to which they call attention remain important clues to its real nature. In the current chapter, I will exploit these clues by working backward from the phenomena to an explanation of why they occur. By asking why we feel and act as we do toward those we blame, we will finally come to see what blame really is.

I

From our reading of Strawson, we learn that blame is often (though not always) accompanied by anger or other negative feelings; while from our reading of the utilitarians, we learn that it is often (though not always) accompanied by behavior, both nonverbal and verbal, that the blamee would prefer to avoid. Taken together, these feelings, actions, and utterances (plus a further class of utterances that are peculiar to self-blame) comprise the data that an adequate theory of blame must explain. Thus, to begin, it will be helpful to review the salient features of the entries on this list.

1. *Anger, etc.* Although we have seen that blame is not always accompanied by hard feelings, there is no denying that it very often is. When we blame someone, we may feel—among other things—anger, resentment, irritation, bitterness, hostility, fury, rage, outrage, disappointment, contempt, disdain, or disgust. Although these feelings differ in important ways, each is always negative and, when it accompanies blame, is always directed at a particular person. In addition, when the feelings arise in connection with blame, each is dependent on a belief that the person at whom it is directed has acted badly or has a bad character. It is a striking and important fact that we immediately relinquish all blame-related bad feeling when we discover that the blamee has a valid excuse, that he did not do the bad thing that we thought he did, or that he does not have the bad trait that we thought he had.

2. *Hostile behavior.* As varied as they are, the negative feelings that accompany blame are circumscribed enough to be describable in a relatively small number of terms. By contrast, the forms of hostile behavior through which we express these feelings cannot be similarly regimented. Our hostile gestures run the gamut from the cut direct to the launching of crockery at an unfaithful spouse. We can display hostility by writing someone out of our will, sending someone a poison-pen letter, sending someone poison, urinating in someone's flower bed, and in indefinitely many other ways. In every case, the way we express our hostility is determined partly by the particulars of our situation, partly by the conventions that determine what count as hostile gestures in situations of that sort, and partly by our own particular mixture of cleverness and caution. Like the anger that they often (but do not always) express, hostile gestures do not manifest blame unless they are rooted in beliefs that the relevant persons have acted badly or have bad characters.

3. *Reproach.* Even when a hostile gesture is rooted in a belief that someone has acted badly or has a bad character, the gesture itself may be fully describable in terms that make no reference to what is believed. This is true, for example, when the gesture consists of a vicious assault

or a gratuitous slur. By contrast, a further class of blame-related acts, whose members are not always carefully distinguished from hostile gestures, are related to the beliefs that sustain them in a much more intimate way. The acts that I have in mind include reproaching, reprimanding, remonstrating, and the like, and what sets them apart from hostile gestures is that they all have intentional objects that make essential reference to what is believed. Unlike a hostile gesture, a reproach is necessarily a reproach *for* something. When we reproach, and *a fortiori* when we pester, hector, nag, berate, or chivy, we always address our interlocutor in a way that alludes to the bad act we take him to have performed or the bad trait we take him to have. Because our allusion is meant to be understood—because the reproach will fall flat if the other person does not know what we are talking about—reproaching someone evidently has a communicative dimension. Just what a reproach is intended to communicate, and just how the intended communication is related to blame itself, are themselves among the questions that an adequate theory of blame must answer.

4. *Apology*. The final blame-related reaction that I will mention, apology, is a manifestation of self-blame rather than blame of another, but is in other respects quite similar to reproach. Like a reprimand but unlike a hostile gesture, every apology is necessarily an apology for something. Like a reprimand, too, an apology is always addressed to another person—in this case, the one we think we have wronged—in a way that alludes to the badness of what has been done. Because this allusion is again meant to be understood—because our apology will fall as flat as our reproach if our interlocutor does not know what we are talking about—apologizing also appears to have a communicative dimension. What we are trying communicate, and how the communication is related to blame itself, are as problematic here as in the case of reproach.

Bearing all this in mind, let us return to the question of what blame adds to a belief that someone has acted badly or has a bad character. (For economy of expression, I will henceforth refer to this belief as "B." Because I will use "B" to designate both a belief-type and its tokens, and because I will take these types and tokens to encompass beliefs about the badness of both acts and traits, this use of "B" will be doubly ambiguous. However, on each occasion, its meaning should be clear from context.) As I hope is now obvious, we cannot take any entry on our list of blame-related reactions, or any combination of those entries, simply to be what blame adds to B. We cannot do this because is perfectly possible to blame someone without being angry at him, without displaying any hostility toward him, without reproaching him, and (in cases of self-blame) without apologizing for what he has done or is. Nevertheless, even when B has no such manifestations, it remains true that anyone who blames someone is at least disposed to become angry at him, to reproach him, and so on. When we blame someone, it is always true that we would do each of these things in many alternative situations. Taking our cue from this, let us now ask what blame's association with these dispositions can tell us about what, beyond B, blame is.[1]

II

One possible answer, appealing in its simplicity, is that the missing element is hiding in plain sight. According to this proposal, what blame adds to B is not something over and above the dispositions to become angry, deliver a reprimand, and so on, but is simply the collection of those dispositions themselves. Instead of taking the missing element to be some further state or event, this proposal takes it to consist precisely of the fact that we would feel anger toward the person whom we blame under one broad set of conditions, would treat him with hostility under another, and would reproach him or apologize for his behavior or character under yet others.

To many philosophers, introducing dispositions in this way is bound to conjure up visions of Rylean behaviorism. Thus, because behaviorism is no longer a live philosophical option, the first thing to say is that the current proposal would not commit us to it. We could

1. After I wrote this section, I discovered that Robert Merrihew Adams had described blame's main manifestations in virtually identical terms. Here is the quotation: "Gibbard understand blame in terms of *feelings* of guilt and resentment. I agree that such feelings are importantly typical of blame, but blaming need not be emotional. Blame can also be constituted by behavior such as reproaching, punishing, and (in cases of self-blame) apologizing" (Robert Merrihew Adams, *Finite and Infinite Goods: A Framework for Ethics* [Oxford: Oxford University Press, 1999], 235–36).

easily take blame to have a dispositional component without implying that the meaning of any (let alone every) mental term can be exhaustively analyzed in terms of some pattern of overt behavior. Indeed, because the current proposal both takes blame essentially to involve a type of belief and takes one of the crucial dispositions to involve a type of feeling, it actually seems inconsistent with any such reductive analysis. And neither, for similar reasons, would accepting the proposal commit us to any particular metaphysical outlook; for the view that blame has a behavioral component is no less compatible with dualism than with any form of physicalism. Thus, whatever else is true, we clearly could accept the current proposal without having to endorse either Ryle's broader analytical ambitions or his particular (anti)metaphysical views.[2]

There are, moreover, some definite advantages *to* accepting this proposal. One point in its favor is that it allows us to square the fact that people can keep their blame entirely to themselves with the intuition that the relation between blame and various forms of overt behavior is too close to be entirely contingent. The way the proposal reconciles blame's privacy with its non-contingent connection to behavior is by taking the relevant forms of overt behavior to be non-contingently connected, not to blame itself, but only to certain dispositions which in their turn are non-contingently connected to blame. And, along similar lines, the proposal allows us to reconcile the often-noticed fact that blame is associated with a singularly rich array of phenomenological manifestations with the seemingly incompatible fact that it has no essential phenomenology of its own. Here again, the key to reconciling

2. Ryle himself is somewhat cagey about the scope of his claims. On the one hand, his rejection of "the dogma of the ghost in the machine" suggests that his commitment to analytical behaviorism is quite general. On the other hand, he seems to acknowledge at least a limited realm of private experiences when he says (e.g.) that "[f]eelings, in any strict sense, are things that come and go or wax and wane in a few seconds; they stab or they grumble; we feel them all over us or else in a particular part" (Gilbert Ryle, *The Concept of Mind* [New York: Barnes and Noble, 1949], 100). On the other hand, again, he seems to withdraw this concession when he says (e.g.) that "we do not, as the prevalent theory holds, act purposively because we experience feelings; we experience feelings, as we wince and shudder, because we are inhibited from acting purposively" (107).

these facts is that the phenomenological manifestations are said to be essential, not to blame itself, but only to certain dispositions which in their turn are essential to blame.

Because it offers these advantages, the dispositional account is in some ways an attractive view. Nevertheless, it is not a view that we can accept. The basic problem is not exactly that it is wrong—I think, in fact, that some affective and behavioral dispositions may indeed be essential to blame—but is rather that it requires augmentation of a kind that renders its reference to these dispositions superfluous. This can be seen in two distinct ways.

One clear indication that more needs to be said is that the reactions in terms of which the dispositions are specified are not related to one another in any obvious way. Considered in themselves, anger, hostile behavior, reproach, and apology are a very mixed group. Their shared connection with blame aside, they have very little in common. Thus, if we were simply to take this collection of dispositions to be what blaming someone adds to believing that he has acted badly or has a bad character, and so on, then we would not be able to explain either why blame merits a single term or why the corresponding concept is morally important. To account for these facts, we will have to move beyond a bare enumeration of the blame-constituting dispositions to an explanation of what unifies them.

There is, moreover, also a further reason to think the dispositional account requires supplementation, and that is that it sheds no light on the relation between B and the dispositions that purportedly transform it into blame. This problem is less apparent than the first because our guiding question—what does blame add to B?—does not imply that there has to be any relation, beyond bare coexistence, between B and blame's additional component. However, although blame could indeed have two unrelated components, it could not possibly have *these* two unrelated components. As I have been at pains to stress, the reactions of anger, hostile behavior, and the rest—and thus, by extension, also the dispositions to have these reactions—are only manifestations of blame when we have them because we hold B. Because of this, the dispositional account cannot possibly assert that what transforms B into blame is simply a collection of dispositions, each of which would exist even if B did not. Instead, to be at all plausible, it must take what transforms B into blame to be a collection of dispositions *each of which exists precisely because B does*.

But once we bring this causal claim into the open, we also bring out a problem about how B itself can give rise to a collection of dispositions. The problem that I have in mind is not that taking B itself to give rise to the dispositions would violate the Humean dictum that beliefs alone can never provide us with motivation. It is, rather, that even those who reject this dictum must concede that B is not always accompanied by all, or even some, of the blame-related dispositions. Given this last fact, it is evidently impossible to account for the existence of the dispositions by simply citing B. To explain why they are present on a given occasion, we must take B to be backed by some further state — perhaps another belief, perhaps not — that combines with it to provide the requisite motivational energy. This means that what the causal version of the dispositional account really takes blame to add to B is not just a certain set of dispositions, but rather a certain set of dispositions *plus whatever further state combines with B to give rise to them*. However, as so amended, the dispositional account not only introduces a competing candidate for the role of the missing element, but also loses much of the elegance and simplicity that initially made it attractive.

All in all, it does not seem plausible to say that what blame adds to B is simply a certain set of affective and behavioral dispositions. However, precisely because this proposal brings out the need for a unifying causal explanation, it also suggests that we may make progress by providing one. To that task, I therefore turn.

III

In general, the preferred strategy for explaining why someone has a number of seemingly disparate dispositions is to take him to have a single goal whose achievement requires that he manifest each disposition in just the circumstances in which he would in fact do so. If we can find the right goal, then we can account for all the things that the person would do by pointing out that they are just the things that we would expect him to do, given various beliefs about his situation, in order to achieve that goal. This is the approach that we take when, to explain why John regularly attends the concerts of bands he knows Mary likes, why John goes out of his way to shop in Mary's neighborhood, and why

John angles for invitations to parties thrown by Mary's friends, we suppose that John's goal is to be around Mary.

There are, of course, different ways of understanding what it is to have such a goal. On a Humean account, which takes all motivation to be supplied by desires or other "passions" that are independent of reason, what moves John to seek Mary's presence is simply that he *wants* to be around Mary.[3] On a non-Humean account, which takes (at least some) motivation to be supplied either by beliefs about what one has reason to do or by desires which in turn are based on such beliefs, John's motivation may stem instead from the fact that he thinks either that there is something good or desirable about his being around Mary or that he has some reason to seek her company.[4] Because my own sympathies lie with Hume (and also because even many anti-Humeans take beliefs about reasons to influence behavior by giving rise to desires[5]), I will couch my own arguments in the language of desire. However, although I shall not pursue the issue, I think parallel arguments may well be available even to those who believe that the sources of motivation can or must be purely cognitive.

By supposing that John wants to be around Mary, we both unify what initially looks like his disparate collection of dispositions and provide a motivational bridge from his beliefs to his actions. These, not coincidentally, are precisely the two problems that the dispositional account of blame was seen to leave unsolved. Thus, the obvious next move is to try to do for blame what we have done for John. If we can trace each blame-related disposition to a single desire, then we will be

3. For Hume's own views on the matter, see the *Treatise of Human Nature*, book II, part III, section III. For an influential contemporary treatment, see Michael Smith, *The Moral Problem* (Oxford: Blackwell, 1994), chapter 4.

4. For defense of this view, see Thomas Nagel, *The Possibility of Altruism* (Oxford: Oxford University Press, 1970); John McDowell, "Are Moral Requirements Hypothetical Imperatives?" *Proceedings of the Aristotelian Society*, Supplementary Volume, 1978: 13–29; Jonathan Dancy, *Moral Reasons* (Oxford: Blackwell, 1993); R. Jay Wallace, "How to Argue About Practical Reason," *Mind* XCIX (July 1990): 355–85; and Thomas Scanlon, *What We Owe to Each Other* (Cambridge, Mass.: Harvard University Press, 1998), chapter 1.

5. See, for example, Nagel, *The Possibility of Altruism* and Wallace, "How to Argue About Practical Reason."

able to explain what those dispositions all have in common; if we can trace them all to a desire that only gives rise to them when backed by B, we will account for their causal dependence upon B. If a single desire can sustain both explanations, it will emerge as the leading candidate for the role of what blame adds to B.

But can a single desire sustain both explanations? Is there in fact a desire that, in conjunction with B, would give rise to each blame-related reaction under roughly the conditions in which we would in fact have it? This is at best not obvious, since our blame-related dispositions are disanalogous to John's Mary-related dispositions in one very important respect: namely, that John's dispositions, but not the ones that we have when we blame people, are activated entirely by beliefs about the future.

For whenever John turns up at the concert of a Mary-favored band, whenever John shops at a supermarket in Mary's neighborhood, and whenever John attends a party given by one of Mary's friends, he does so precisely because he thinks it likely (enough) that Mary will be there. Each such belief, being about the future, is capable of meshing with, and thus triggering, John's standing future-oriented desire to be with Mary.

However, and in stark contrast, the beliefs that sustain the dispositions that are characteristic of blame are *never* oriented to the future. What we believe when we have these dispositions is always either that someone has acted badly already or that someone has a bad trait right now. Because each instance of B is oriented exclusively to the past or present, B does not seem capable of meshing with any future-oriented desire in a way that could account for our blame-related dispositions.

This does not mean that we cannot trace all of the blame-related dispositions to a single desire, but it does mean we can only do so by showing that the relevant desire and whatever belief(s) we take to combine with it are oriented in the same temporal direction. To bring our desire-belief pair into alignment, we could argue either that (a) despite appearances, the beliefs that combine with the relevant desire are really forward-looking, or else that (b) despite appearances, the relevant desire itself is really not forward-looking. Let us consider each possibility in turn.

Because our beliefs about what a person did or would do are often the basis for expectations about what he will do, the obvious way to implement the first strategy is to take B to give rise to a belief about the future via an inductive inference. On this account, the unifying explanation of our blame-related dispositions consists, first, of the claim that holding B about a person leads us to expect him to act badly (again) in the future, and, second, of the claim that this expectation combines with our desire that he not act badly (again) to dispose us to take deterrent action. Because we expect the future to be like the past, we may view each blame-related disposition as traceable to the combination of a future-oriented expectation of bad conduct and an equally future-oriented desire to forestall such conduct.

But, for several reasons, this will not do. At the most abstract level, the reason we cannot accept the proposal is that assigning our beliefs about people's past transgressions and present vices a purely evidential role would mean assimilating blame to the purely forward-looking reactions that Pereboom correctly views as alternatives to blame. In addition, and more concretely, this way of unifying the blame-constituting dispositions would not explain why we are sometimes disposed to react with anger, hostility, and so on, even to wrongdoers and bad people whose future behavior poses no threat—for example, to persons who are incapacitated or distant or dead. And yet a further objection, if any is needed, is that two of the four main blame-related reactions—namely, feeling (as opposed to manifesting) anger and apologizing for one's own misbehavior—are in fact not effective strategies for preventing wrongdoers and bad people from acting badly (again) in the future, and so can hardly be intended to achieve that aim.

Because these objections are so powerful, the strategy of taking the relevant beliefs to be oriented to the future holds little promise. Thus, if we are to succeed in tracing each blame-related disposition to a desire-belief pair whose members are oriented in the same direction, it will have to be by adopting the alternative strategy of taking the relevant desires to be oriented to the past or present. To explain why we are disposed to react to those whom we take to have acted badly by becoming angry at them, treating them with hostility, reproaching them, and, in cases of self-blame, apologizing for what they have done, we will have to trace each reaction to the single backward-looking desire that the person *not have done* what he in fact did. And, analogously, to explain why we are disposed to react in these ways to persons we take to have bad characters, we will have to trace each reaction to the single present-tense desire that the person's character not be as bad as it in fact is.

I will turn to an examination of this proposal shortly. However, before I do, I want to introduce one additional bit of terminology. Corresponding to my use of "B" to designate the belief that a person has acted badly or has a bad character, I will use the term "D" to designate the desire that the person not have acted badly or not have a bad character. Like my use of "B," my use of "D" will be doubly ambiguous; for it will range both over types of desires and over tokens of those types, and will in addition be used to designate desires whose propositional objects involve both acts and traits. However, also like "B," "D" will on each occasion be disambiguated by the context in which it is employed.

Can we account for each blame-related disposition by attributing it to the combination of B and D? By adopting this strategy, we would avoid both the objection that the members of our desire-belief pair cannot mesh because they face in different temporal directions and the objection that they are too exclusively forward-looking to shed any real light on blame. However, in so doing, we would also reraise a version of the very difficulty that the introduction of a unifying desire was supposed to get us beyond. Simply put, the resurgent difficulty is that in taking the relevant desires to be oriented exclusively to the past or present, we appear to strip them of their capacity to motivate. We are often moved to act on future-oriented desires because we often think we can affect what happens in the future. However, because no one believes he can change the past, it is unclear how any desire (or, more accurately, any wish) that someone not have acted badly in the past can combine with any further belief to give rise to any (further) action now. Analogously, because we all know that character does not change instantly, it is unclear how any desire that someone not have a bad trait right now can combine with any belief to give rise to any action either. In each case, our perceived impotence renders it unclear how D can provide us with any motivation at all. Thus, *a fortiori*, it is unclear how D can provide us with enough motivation to account for all the dispositions that are associated with blame.

IV

But, for all that, it can; for even when we have no way of translating our desires into effective plans of actions, we may still be moved by them in a variety of ways. We may, in particular, still be moved to

1. feel badly about not getting what we want; or
2. publicly express our unsatisfied desire; or
3. substitute the pursuit of some related but more achievable goal.

Although none of these reactions are aimed at satisfying the original desire—some, indeed, are not purposive actions at all—each is, in a clear sense, nevertheless still motivated *by* that desire.

Thus, properly understood, the real question that the current proposal raises is not whether D can provide us with enough motivation to account for all of our blame-related dispositions, but only whether the motivation it can provide is of the right sort. Does the hypothesis that we have D illuminate our actual reactions to those whom we take to have acted badly or to have bad characters? Can what D would motivate us to do be shown to match up with what we are disposed to do when we blame such people?

There is, as far as I can see, no single way to link D to all four types of blame-related disposition; but neither can I see why the linkage must be the same in all four cases. To establish that all four dispositions have a common source, what we need to show is not that all of them stem from the same desire in the same way, but only that all of them stem from the same desire in one way or another. Moreover, when we approach the problem in this more relaxed spirit, we find that all four types of disposition can indeed be traced to D; for anger and hostile behavior are pretty clearly reactions of type (1), while reproach and apology can be seen to combine elements of (2) and (3).

It is no accident that the word "frustration" designates both the thwarting of a desire and a type of negative feeling; for feelings of frustration very often accompany frustrated desires. These feelings can, of course, vary greatly—compare, for example, the way it feels when our team fritters away a large lead, when our career aspirations are set back, when our romantic aspirations are set back, and when we have trouble following complicated assembly directions. However, for present purposes, what matters is not that these feelings are so varied but only that they are all negative.

Just why the motivational energy that is latent in unsatisfied desires should regularly discharge itself in bad feelings is not something a philosopher can explain. It is simply a brute fact of human psychology. However, precisely because it *is* a fact, the obvious way to invoke D to account for our disposition to become angry at those we blame is to assimilate that anger to the other negative feelings that we have when we see that we cannot get what we want. Just as obviously, the way to invoke D to account for our disposition to display hostility toward those we blame is to see our hostile behavior as a natural expression of our negative feelings toward them.

Let me be more specific about what I am proposing. As I have suggested, the basic strategy is to exploit the pervasive connection between failing to get what we want and having negative feelings. However, to implement that strategy convincingly, I must explain why our inability to satisfy D leads not to the generalized frustration that we feel when we get stuck in traffic or botch a plumbing repair, but rather to bad feelings that are directed specifically at the wrongdoer or bad person himself. I must also explain why these person-specific bad feelings can take so many different forms—why our list includes anger, resentment, irritation, bitterness, and the rest. Because it is impossible to explain why unsatisfied desires give rise to bad feeling at all, it is, in one sense, also impossible to explain why they issue in just the bad feelings they do. However, what can be done, and what may be sufficient for our purposes, is to bring out certain facts about D in light of which the particulars of the relevant bad feelings are at least not surprising.

To see why it would not be surprising if the thwarting of D were to lead to bad feelings that are directed at the wrongdoer or bad person, we need only remind ourselves of the peculiarly close connection between that person and what is wanted. When we have an unsatisfiable desire to escape a traffic jam or fix a broken drain, we may indeed want other people to act in certain ways (e.g. pull over and let us pass, do the repair for us), but we want this only because it would produce a further result that does not essentially involve them. By contrast, when we have an unsatisfiable desire that someone not have acted badly or not have a bad character, our desire is directed at that person not merely in the superficial sense that we want something that he could bring about, nor yet in the somewhat deeper sense that we want something that we cannot fully describe without mentioning him, but rather in the deepest sense that we want him to have exercised his own decision-making capacities in a certain way. Because what we want is that he have responded, or that he be disposed to respond, to what we consider a compelling moral reason, we cannot even bring what we want into clear focus without projecting ourselves into his perspective and imagining ourselves making a decision that he did not make or is not disposed to make.[6] Because the thwarted desire is itself in this way focused on him, it will hardly be surprising if, when its blocked emotional energy goes over into bad feelings, those feelings retain the desire's original focus.

Nor, further, should we be surprised that those feelings are so varied; for the differences among them are strongly correlated with differences in the circumstances in which they arise. Thus, to cite just four examples, the felt difference between indignation and resentment mirrors the fact that indignation is elicited by wrongs done to others, resentment by wrongs done to us; the felt difference between contempt and both indignation and resentment corresponds to the fact that contempt is elicited by bad traits, indignation and resentment by bad acts; the fact that the blame-related feelings can range from mild irritation to unbridled rage corresponds to the facts that people differ in how emotional they are, in how much they care about morality, and in the degree to which they are distracted by other concerns; and the fact that we react to wrongdoers sometimes only with hostility, at other times also with disappointment, corresponds to the fact that we sometimes, but not always, expected better from them.

Although the introduction of these circumstantial factors does not explain why our negative feelings about wrongdoers and bad people have the exact qualities that they do, it does provide the materials for a schematic explanation of why they differ. In this way, it allows us to accommodate the variation among those feelings without relinquishing the basic idea that each is a result of D's frustration. Combined with the previous points, this suggests that adding D to B does allow us to explain what are sometimes called the "retributive emotions."

It is, however, one thing to say that D provides an explanation of the retributive emotions, and quite another to say that it provides the best explanation. Thus, before I turn to D's relations to the remaining

---

6. Compare Thomas Nagel: "When we hold the defendant responsible, the result is not merely a description of his character, but a vicarious occupation of his point of view and evaluation of his action from within it" (Thomas Nagel, *The View from Nowhere* [Oxford: Oxford University Press, 1986], 121).

blame-related dispositions, I want briefly to contrast the explanation I have just proposed with its most famous rival. The alternative explanation that I have in mind is, of course, Nietzsche's. According to Nietzsche, the anger and other negative emotions that we feel toward wrongdoers are expressions of *ressentiment*—a complex attitude that includes both our fear of those who are strong and strong-willed and our envy of their success at flouting moral prohibitions that we dare not violate.[7] On Nietzsche's account, the ultimate source of the retributive emotions is not our allegiance to morality but rather our sense of our own weakness and inadequacy.[8] When Nietzsche traces our blame-related anger to fear and envy, it is not entirely clear whether he is speaking only of a (possible or actual) past stage in the history of the development of our (individual or collective) psychology, or whether he wants to say that all instances of wrongdoing currently evoke (hidden) fear or envy in many (members of the herd) who are aware of them.[9] However, even if Nietzsche is making some version of the latter claim, there will remain two reasons why his insightful account poses little threat to what has been said here.

For, first, even if we grant that fear and envy are the ultimate sources of the anger that we feel toward wrongdoers, it hardly follows that that anger cannot also be traced to D's frustration. The reason this does not follow is that Nietzsche's larger aim in invoking the fear and envy that the weak feel toward the strong is precisely to explain why the weak want the

7. See Friedrich Nietzsche, *On the Genealogy of Morals*, trans. Walter Kaufmann (New York: Vintage, 1969); and Friedrich Nietzsche, *Thus Spoke Zarathustra*, trans. Walter Kaufmann (New York: Viking, 1954).

8. A variation on this theme, recently proposed by Jean Hampton, is that our anger at the wrongdoer reflects a need to shore up our own self-esteem when we take ourselves to have been wronged; see Jean Hampton, "Forgiveness, Resentment, and Hatred," in Jeffrie G. Murphy and Jean Hampton, *Forgiveness and Mercy* (Cambridge: Cambridge University Press, 1988), 35–87. For an interesting discussion of Nietzsche's account of the retributive emotions, see Michael Moore, *Placing Blame* (Oxford: Oxford University Press, 1997), chapter 3.

9. For discussion of the significance of genealogies (including, but not restricted to, Nietzsche's), see Bernard Williams, *Truth and Truthfulness* (Princeton, N.J.: Princeton University Press, 2002), esp. chapter 2.

strong to be hamstrung by moral principles—the very sorts of principles at whose non-violation D is directed. Given this larger aim, the obvious way to reconcile the Nietzschean claim that the retributive emotions are rooted in fear and envy with the current claim that they are caused by D's frustration is to say that our fear and envy of the strong give rise to the retributive emotions precisely by causing us to *have* desires like D.

But neither, second, is it really clear that fear and envy always *are* the ultimate sources of the retributive emotions. Against this claim, it may be argued that we often have such emotions even toward persons whom we seem neither to envy nor to fear. We can be absolutely furious at someone whom we blame even though he is too weak or remote from us to pose any threat; can feel disgust or contempt for someone whose behavior or character we find pitiable rather than enviable; and can be indignant toward a wrongdoer whose transgressions will affect only others. Because such cases are so common, attributing all blame-related bad feelings to *ressentiment* would mean postulating hidden fear or envy in many contexts in which none is apparent. By contrast, because it is clear enough that anyone who is angry at someone he blames does wish that that person had not acted badly or did not have a bad character, the claim that our blame-related bad feelings stem from D's frustration requires no comparably extravagant hypothesis. Hence, on grounds of simple parsimony, the explanation proposed here seems markedly preferable.

V

So far, I have argued that two sorts of blame-related disposition—the dispositions to have bad feelings about, and to display hostility toward, the persons whom we take to have acted badly or to have bad characters—can be understood as instances of the familiar affective and behavioral tendencies that are known to accompany the frustration of our desires. However, the remaining two blame-related dispositions—to apologize for our own transgressions and vices and to reproach others for theirs—require different treatment. We cannot trace these reactions to the bad feelings that often accompany our failure to get what we want because reprimands and apologies are neither bad feelings themselves nor always accompanied by them. It is true that many apologies are backed by remorse and many reprimands delivered with heat; but it is also true that these connections are far from universal. We can both apologize and reprimand others without feeling anything at all. Hence, if these dispositions, too, are to be traced to the unsatisfiable D, then the way it gives rise to them will have to be either by motivating its own expression or by motivating its possessor to pursue some alternative goal.

At first glance, the suggestion that D might give rise to the dispositions by motivating its own expression may not seem promising; for we often have an incentive not to publicize our unsatisfied desires. We generally (and rightly) expect others to find our wish lists tiresome. However, because D is a specifically moral desire—because it is directed at the non-existence of a bad act or trait—we also have at least two positive reasons for going public with it. For one thing, by doing so, we both reaffirm to ourselves and make clear to others the broader commitment to morality in which D is rooted—a reaffirmation and clarification that is often called for by that very commitment itself. For another, by failing to make D public, we risk becoming complicit in the very transgression or vice whose non-existence we desire.[10] For both reasons, D seems far more likely than other unsatisfiable desires to motivate its own expression.

And, because it is, one way to show that D provides a motivational bridge between B and our dispositions to apologize for our own moral failures and to reproach others for theirs is simply to point out that (sincere) reproaches and apologies both *do* involve public expressions of D. When we reproach someone for acting badly, we make it clear that if it were up to us, he would not have done so; when we reproach someone for having a bad character, we make known our desire that he not have such a character; and when we apologize for our own bad behavior or character, we imply that we would change what we have done or what we are if we now could. Because apologizing and reprimanding are both ways of making it clear that we want the relevant bad act or trait not to (have) exist(ed), one obvious explanation of why we are disposed to do these things is precisely that we are motivated publicly to express that very desire.

<hr />

10. For illuminating discussion of complicity, see Clint Parker, *Complicity* (Rice University doctoral dissertation, 2002).

But this cannot be the only, or even the main, explanation of why we have these dispositions; for by itself, it sheds no light on why we are disposed to express D through the performance of the complicated speech acts of apologizing and reprimanding rather than through the less complicated medium of unadorned optative utterance. If all that we're trying to do is make others aware that we have D, then why don't we just say so? If we are to bring D to bear in a way that avoids this question, then we will have to appeal to the last of the three things that an unsatisfiable desire can motivate us to do—namely, to replace its object with some related but more achievable goal.

We have all had the experience of pursuing a goal because it has something in common with what we really want but know we cannot get. We do this whenever we lower our sights—when, for example, we try to salvage second place in a race we can no longer win or abandon our efforts to impress in favor of damage control. There are, to be sure, interesting questions about how best to describe the relation between an unsatisfiable desire and the action it motivates—about whether, for example, we should say that the now-unsatisfiable desire to win the race (a) is itself what motivates us to try to come in second, or (b) gives rise to a further desire to come in second that in turn motivates us, or (c) was always only the initial disjunct of more complex desire (to finish first, or, failing that, second, or failing that, third . . .), the second disjunct of which has now kicked in. However, whichever description we choose, there is obviously *some* way in which an unsatisfiable desire can move us to pursue a goal that only partly resembles its object. Thus, for present purposes, the only real question is whether what we can hope to accomplish by issuing an apology or a reprimand is sufficiently similar to the object of the unsatisfiable D to account for the transfer of motivation from D's object to it.

And, upon inspection, it pretty clearly is; for even if a wrongdoer can no longer act on the situation-specific moral reason that he has ignored or flouted, it remains possible for him to come to appreciate in retrospect—and thus also for someone else to bring him to appreciate in retrospect—the force of the very moral reason that he ignored or flouted in prospect. *Mutatis mutandis*, something similar holds for a bad person; for although he cannot undo his current lack of responsiveness to the relevant type of moral reason, he can at least come to see what is wrong with it. If a wrongdoer or a bad person does thus come to see the error of his ways, his doing so will not satisfy the relevant D; but it will resemble the (impossible) outcome that would satisfy D in that (a) each will be an event in the life of the same temporally extended person, and (b) in each case, that person will respond appropriately to the same situation-specific moral reason or type of moral reason. This, surely, is a close enough resemblance to qualify the relevant form of retrospective recognition as the sort of second-best outcome that a person with D might be motivated to seek.

However, if so, then the final pieces of the puzzle will fall into place. To explain why those who blame others are disposed to reprimand them, and why those who blame themselves are disposed to apologize, we can now point out that reprimands and apologies are both ways of achieving what those with D must regard as the best available alternative outcomes. The ways in which apologizing and reproaching are related to these outcomes are, of course, not the same, since an apology is itself a retrospective response to the (type of) moral reason that the agent has flouted in prospect, while a reprimand is merely an attempt to elicit such a response in another.

Nevertheless, despite this difference, both reactions are recognizably motivated by D. By demonstrating through our apology our current responsiveness to the (type of) moral reason that we now wish we had not previously flouted, we come as close as we still can to satisfying the reflexive version of D; while by trying through our reproach to elicit a similar responsiveness in another, we seek an aim which, if we achieve it, will bring us as close as we can still come to satisfying D's non-reflexive version.[11] Because these last two blame-constituting dispositions are thus also rendered intelligible by D, we may conclude that D is indeed an essential element of blame.

11. Of course, despite our best rhetorical and persuasive efforts, most wrongdoers can be expected to remain indifferent to the moral reasons they have flouted and most bad people can be expected to remain indifferent to their own corruption. However, what matters for the current argument is not what our reproaches in fact accomplish but only what they aim at.

VI

This completes my discussion of what blaming someone adds to believing that he has acted badly or is a bad person. The additional element, I have argued, is a set of affective and behavioral dispositions, each of which can be traced to the single desire that the person in question not have performed his past bad act or not have his current bad character. But how much of this additional element is essential to blame and how much is merely contingently associated with it? To arrive at the best version of my proposal, should I take the blame itself to encompass only the central desire-belief pair or also the various dispositions that that pair supports?

If my aim were either to analyze the concept of blame or to define the word "blame," then the answer would depend on what we would say about a person who had a desire-belief pair of the relevant kind but lacked the corresponding dispositions. It would depend on whether we would describe X as blaming Y if X believed that Y had acted badly, X wanted Y not to have acted badly, but had a psychology that was so nonstandard that he lacked any of the affective or behavioral dispositions that normally accompany such desires and beliefs. For the record, I do not think we would be willing to describe X as blaming Y under these conditions; but for present purposes, this does not matter. Instead, what matters is that such cases are so nonstandard that our intuitions about them are simply irrelevant. The intuitions are irrelevant because the focus of our inquiry is neither a word nor a concept but a phenomenon in the world. We have all had the experience of blaming others and being blamed by them, and what we are trying to find out is what such blame amounts to. Because my topic is the nature of blame itself—because I am seeking neither a conceptual analysis nor a dictionary definition but something more akin to a theory—the natural way to approach it is to ask what could fill the causal and normative role that we know blame to occupy. That is the question to which "a set of dispositions organized around a central desire-belief pair" is my answer. Because the point of including the dispositions is simply to explain why blame has the characteristics it does, this answer will work equally well if we take the dispositions to be essential to blame and if we take them to be merely its (virtually) universal effects. Thus, as long as every actual person who has a desire-belief pair of the relevant sort also has most, if not all, of the relevant dispositions, we need not worry about imaginary people who have the desire-belief pairs without the dispositions.

Should we then accept the proposed account? Because I have worked my way to it by asking how we can improve on its main competitors, we may confidently assert that it makes good their deficiencies while preserving their advantages. Unlike Smart's view that blame is simply a form of social control, my proposal captures the fact that blame can be kept private; unlike Zimmerman's view that blame is a combination of beliefs, it explains why blaming and not being blamed matter to us as much as they do; unlike the affective accounts of Strawson and his followers, it comfortably accommodates the fact that blame need not involve either any hostility or any withdrawal of good will. At the same time, the current account preserves what is attractive about each rival—for example, the utilitarians' insight that we can and often do influence people's behavior by letting them know that we blame them, and the Strawsonians' observation that we often withdraw good will from, and feel anger toward, the persons we blame. It is, thus, a good theory in the sense of allowing us to explain a broad range of relevant phenomena.[12]

Nevertheless, the discussion to this point is far from conclusive; for an important range of questions remains to be addressed. As I remarked

12. Does the theory also shed light on the important blame-related phenomenon of forgiveness? At first glance, it may seem not to; for if forgiving someone consists precisely of renouncing one's blame, as is commonly assumed, then my claim that blaming someone involves both believing that he has acted badly or has a bad character and wanting this not be the case will imply that forgiving someone involves renouncing either the relevant belief or the relevant desire. This implication is problematic because it is unclear either what these forms of renunciation would amount to or why there is anything desirable about either one. However, to avoid the problematic implication, we need only restrict the renunciation of which forgiveness consists to the dispositions in blame's second tier. When we do, we arrive at the satisfying view that to forgive someone is still to believe that he has acted badly or has a bad character, is still to want him not to have acted badly or not to have a bad character, but is no longer to be disposed either to feel or manifest anger toward him or to say things intended draw his attention to his moral shortcomings.

at the outset, blame and blameworthiness are correlative notions. Thus, any adequate account of blame must allow us to make sense of the idea that blame is something of which a wrongdoer or bad person can be worthy. Making sense of blameworthiness does not mean showing that anyone actually is blameworthy—hard determinists, after all, must be able to make sense of it, too—but it does at least require a convincing account of what blameworthiness would amount to if it existed. As I put the point earlier, no account of blame is adequate unless it slides smoothly into the groove that blameworthiness reserves for it.

This is not an easy test to pass; the neo-Strawsonian account, for one, has been seen not to pass it. Thus, one unresolved question is whether my own account can do better. A further unresolved question is whether, if my account of blame does allow us to make sense of blameworthiness, the resulting integrated account sheds light on what blame and blameworthiness mean to us—on their relation to the other elements of our moral scheme and their role in our interpersonal economy. These, of course, are the questions with which we began, and it is fitting that we end by returning to them.

SEVEN

IN PRAISE OF BLAME

IN THIS, THE BOOK'S LAST CHAPTER, I WILL DO TWO THINGS. FIRST, TO complete the argument I began in the previous chapter, I will explain why blame as I understand it is something of which a wrongdoer or bad person can be worthy. Second, to answer the larger question around which the book is structured, I will explain why the blame that we direct at wrongdoers and bad people is inseparable from our commitment to morality itself. Though pitched at different levels, the two explanations will turn out to be connected; for it is precisely by clarifying what makes blame appropriate in particular cases that we will come to see why it is central to our moral lives.

I

To blame someone, I have argued, is to have certain affective and behavioral dispositions, each of which can be traced to the combination of a belief that that person has acted badly or has a bad character and a desire that this not be the case. Thus, to show that blame as so conceived is something of which a wrongdoer or bad person can be worthy, I will have to explain how his bad act or trait can render appropriate a suitable combination of these elements. Just which elements are involved, and what "appropriate" might mean when applied to them, are, of course, crucial aspects of what needs to be explained.

Because we recognize blame primarily through its affective and behavioral manifestations, one obvious way to approach the question of why it is appropriate is to ask which norms might justify the relevant feelings and actions. However, despite their early salience, our dispositions to react to those we blame by getting mad at them, reproaching them, and the rest have turned out to be of secondary importance. As we saw, those dispositions are causally dependent on, and are unified only by their common origins in, the relevant beliefs and desires. Because the beliefs and desires are clearly prior, I will, for the most part, restrict my attention to them. If we can explain why they are called for, the dispositions they sustain should pose few additional problems.

There is a venerable tradition according to which even a true belief does not count as knowledge unless the person who holds it has good reason to do so. This tradition presupposes that there are norms that tell in favor of accepting some beliefs and against accepting others. Thus, given that blame essentially involves a belief that someone has acted badly or is a bad person, one possible way of understanding how blame can be called for is to invoke these justificatory norms. When we do, we arrive at the view that what renders someone blameworthy is simply the fact that people are (or would be) justified in holding blame-constituting beliefs about him.

But, whatever else is true, this cannot be right. One obvious reason to reject the proposal is that people are not all justified in believing the same things. Because what any given person is justified in believing depends on his evidence, his background beliefs, and perhaps other things, the current proposal would imply that an agent can be blameworthy relative to the situations of some people but not blameworthy relative to the situations of others. This implication is problematic because blameworthiness appears to be a status that a person either has or does not.

In addition, even if we could somehow sidestep the problematic implication (for example, by stipulating that a person counts as blame-worthy *simpliciter* as long as a large enough number of people, or a suitably large ratio of them, are justified in believing that he has acted badly or has a bad character), the proposal would remain vulnerable to the deeper objection that a person's being justified in believing something is no guarantee that it is true. Because justification and truth can come apart, it is perfectly possible for the vast majority of people to be justified in believing that a certain person has acted badly or has a bad character when in fact his behavior and character are impeccable. In such a case, the current proposal would imply that the person is blameworthy; but in fact, he clearly would not be.

Epistemologists disagree about whether (and if so why) the features of a belief that count toward its justification also raise the likelihood that it is true; but most would agree that we want our beliefs to be justified *because* we want them to be true. Moreover, quite apart from questions about justification, truth is often said to be the aim of belief.[1] Taking our cue from this, let us next consider the possibility that what renders blame appropriate is indeed a norm that governs beliefs, but that what that norm requires is not that beliefs be justified but that they be true. Let us consider, in other words, the proposal that what renders a wrong-doer or a bad person blameworthy is simply the fact that his behavior or character makes true the blame-constituting belief that he has acted badly or is a bad person — a belief that, if backed by a desire that he not have acted badly or not be a bad person, would in its turn give rise to precisely the dispositions that are characteristic of blame.[2]

This proposal is a definite step forward. By shifting from a norm that requires that our beliefs be justified to one that requires that they be true, we can avoid both the unacceptable implication that a person can be blameworthy relative to some people but not to others and the equally unacceptable implication that what renders a person blameworthy need not have anything to do with the badness of what he has

---

1. For subtle discussion of the view that the built-in goal of belief is to represent reality accurately, see David Velleman, "On the Aim of Belief," in his *The Possibility of Practical Reason* (Oxford: Oxford University Press, 2000), 244–81. For a dissenting view, see Nishi Shah, "How Truth Governs Belief," *The Philosophical Review* 112 (October 2003): 447–82.

2. Compare R. Jay Wallace: "It is a condition of moral blameworthiness for a given action . . . that the action violates some moral obligation that we accept. But why is this a condition of blameworthiness for a given action? The account just sketched traces the answer to our theoretical interest in the truth: to hold s responsible for x is (in part) to believe that x has violated a moral obligation we accept, and this belief would be false if x did not in fact violate a moral obligation of this kind" (R. Jay Wallace, *Responsibility and the Moral Sentiments* [Cambridge, Mass.: Harvard University Press, 1994], 134).

done or is. In addition, by taking blame to be appropriate when and because its belief-component is true, we can nicely explain why various excuses render blame inappropriate.

The obvious explanation here is that the belief upon whose truth the appropriateness of blame depends—the belief that the agent has acted badly in the sense of flouting or ignoring a compelling moral reason—is rendered false by each of the standard excuses. We standardly take someone to have an excuse when he could not be expected to know that his act would have the feature that made it wrong; when he caused harm inadvertently, by accident or because he lacked control over his movements; when he acted wrongly because he was very tired or disoriented or ill or in shock; when he did so because he is retarded or brain damaged; and when he was acting under (a sufficiently severe form of) coercion or duress. In each such case, the excusing factor establishes that the agent either could not recognize or could not respond effectively to the moral reasons for not doing what he did. This shows that he neither ignored nor flouted those reasons because an agent can only ignore a reason that he knows to exist and can only flout a reason to which he has the capacity to respond.[3] Hence, if what renders someone blameworthy is simply the (potential) truth of a belief that he has ignored or flouted a

---

3. There are, of course, many unresolved questions about how to draw the distinction between an agent who is incapable of recognizing or responding to the moral reasons that his situations provides and one who simply ignores or flouts those reasons. One such question is on which side of the line we should locate a clear-headed, rational, well-coordinated, uncoerced sociopath. Do the mental abilities that he shares with the rest of us warrant our describing his lack of responsiveness to moral reasons as ignoring or flouting, or does his systematic insensitivity to those reasons itself bespeak a lack of (real) access? Another question, less dramatic but more important, is what to say about the person who acts wrongly because he lacks moral imagination, has bad judgment, or simply fails to notice some morally relevant feature of his situation. Fortunately, these questions are not ones we need to resolve; for any uncertainties about whether a given sociopath or moral dullard was in a position to recognize and respond to the moral reasons upon which he failed to act are precisely matched by uncertainties about whether he is *blameworthy*. Because the two sets of uncertainties coincide, the manifest unclarity of the distinction between lacking access to a moral reason and ignoring or flouting it not only does not undermine the claim that blameworthiness requires ignoring or flouting, but is if anything a point in its favor.

moral reason, then our unwillingness to consider an agent blameworthy when he has a valid excuse is only to be expected.

Given all this, there is clearly something right about the claim that what makes blame appropriate is the (potential) truth of the relevant blame-constituting belief. Still, if the sense in which blame is appropriate were merely that in which any belief is appropriate to the facts that make it true, then the claim that a wrongdoer or bad person is blameworthy would be precisely on a par with the claim that (e.g.) a white cat is worthy of being judged white. This cannot be all that blameworthiness involves because the status of blameworthiness is morally significant in a way that the status of being worthy of being judged white is not. The claim that a cat is worthy of being judged white is simply a roundabout way of saying that the cat *is* white, but the claim that a person is blameworthy is not just a roundabout way of saying that the person has flouted or ignored, or is disposed to flout or ignore, a certain (type of) moral reason. Just what the attribution of blameworthiness adds is, of course, what we are trying to establish, but whatever it is, it clearly goes far beyond the truth of the relevant belief. Because our current proposal fails to capture this further element, it is, by itself, far too weak to be credible.

II

To see whether the proposal can be strengthened, let us turn next from norms of belief to norms of desire. To blame someone, I have argued, is not just to believe that he has acted badly or has a bad character, but is also to want him not to have acted badly or not to have a bad character. Even if each such desire presupposes the corresponding belief, it is clear that the desires go essentially beyond the beliefs. Thus, the natural next question is what makes the desires themselves appropriate. By answering this question, we may hope both to preserve our previous gains and to capture the elusive sense in which blame is morally important.

Why is it appropriate to want someone not to have acted badly or not to have a bad character? In what value, obligation, or other norm might the appropriateness of such a desire be grounded? Because each blame-constituting desire is directed at the nonexistence of some bad act or trait, the most straightforward answer to this question is that what makes such desires appropriate is simply the badness of the relevant acts and traits. Because it is good when people are responsive to moral reasons and bad when they are not, why not simply attribute the appropriateness of a desire that a wrongdoer not have ignored or flouted a given moral reason, or that a bad person not be disposed to ignore or flout a given type of moral reason, to whatever reasons we have to want what happens to be good rather than bad?

I think, in fact, that this proposal contains a good deal of truth. However, I also think that in its current form, the proposal is vulnerable to two serious objections. First, and most obviously, it rests on the undefended assumption that our reasons for wanting things not to go badly extend to the past and present as well as the future. It assumes that we have reason not only to want bad things not to happen tomorrow, but also to want them not to have happened yesterday and not to be happening today. This last assumption is problematic because a reason to want a bad thing not to have happened in the past, or not to be happening right now, would have to be a curious hybrid. On the one hand, it would presumably be a practical rather than a theoretical reason, since whatever else it was, it clearly would not be a reason for holding any belief. However, on the other hand, it would at best be a very *impractical* practical reason, since unlike a reason to want something bad not to happen in the future, it could not possibly be a reason to try to bring about what it was a reason for wanting. Given the odd, intermediate nature of the reasons to which the current proposal must appeal, the claim that such reasons exist is clearly in need of defense.

And there is also another problem with the proposal: namely, that as stated it does not distinguish moral from nonmoral (dis)value. Because its guiding premise is simply that we have reason to want any bad past event not to have occurred, the proposal runs together our reasons for wanting people not to have acted badly or to have bad characters and our reasons for wanting events whose badness had nothing to do with wrongdoing— illnesses, bitter divorces, earthquakes, and the like—not to have taken place or not to be occurring now. Because it blurs the distinction between these two forms of disvalue, the proposal threatens to assimilate the appropriateness of the sorts of desire-belief combinations with which I have identified blame to the appropriateness of the combination of (say) a true belief that someone has had a bad case of shingles and a desire that he not have suffered so much pain. An account with such implications, however, would be radically deflationary: as so understood, blameworthiness would not be a fundamental moral category.

Can we refine our proposal in a way that avoids these objections? If we can, the refinement will have to turn on some factor that is associated exclusively with *moral* badness. As we saw, what makes an act morally bad is that the agent has ignored or flouted a (sufficiently weighty) moral reason not to perform it, while what makes a trait morally bad is that its possessor is disposed to ignore or flout a particular type of moral reason. Thus, the natural place to begin is with the linkage between moral badness and moral reasons. This linkage is potentially relevant to both objections: to the first because moral reasons are themselves practical reasons, and to the second because moral reasons play no comparable role in determining the badness of illnesses, failed marriages, or natural disasters. But how, if at all, can we exploit the linkage between moral reasons and moral badness to show that the moral badness of a past act or a present trait gives us a unique sort of practical reason to want it not to have been performed or not to exist?

To answer this question, we will have to take a step back from the moral reasons whose ignoring, flouting, and so on, has been seen to render past acts and present traits bad, and focus instead on the broader moral principles that provide us with such reasons.[4] The advantage of taking this backward step is that it brings into view both the deeper considerations that give us reason to accept the relevant moral principles and the full range of commitments that accepting those principles involves. By attending simultaneously to these deeper reasons and this range of commitments, we will open up the possibility of defending the inference from "X has ignored or flouted a moral reason" to "We have reason to want X not to have done so" (and the corresponding inference from "X is disposed to ignore or flout a type of moral reason" to "We have reason to want X not to be so disposed") by showing that X's

4. To speak of moral reasons as supplied by principles is simply to acknowledge the truism that any feature of a person's situation that gives him a reason to act in a certain way must also provide reasons to perform other similar acts in other (sufficiently) similar situations. For illuminating discussion of the complexities that this truism conceals, see Thomas Scanlon, *What We Owe to Each Other* (Cambridge, Mass.: Harvard University Press, 1998), 197–202.

reasons and our own have a common source. We will, in other words, open up the possibility of arguing that the reasons for acting on moral principles and for wanting their requirements not to have gone unmet come as a package deal: that because fully accepting a moral principle involves wanting those who have violated it not to have done so and those who are disposed to violated it not to be so disposed, any consideration that gives us reason to accept (and therefore act on) such a principle must also give us reason to have the corresponding past- and present-oriented desires.

In what follows, I will advance an argument of this general sort. In so doing, I will draw on a connection that has been explored with great subtlety by Bernard Williams. Like Williams, I believe that the urge to blame is bound up with a commitment to morality itself—that "blame is the characteristic reaction of the morality system";[5] and like Williams, too, I believe that this linkage is consistent with many different reconstructions of morality's substantive content. However, because Williams takes blame to impose requirements that cannot coherently be met,[6] he sees the fact that morality requires blame as a reason to reject the "peculiar institution" of morality. By contrast, because I don't think blame is incoherent but do think we have good reason to embrace morality, I want to

5. Bernard Williams, *Ethics and the Limits of Philosophy* (Cambridge, Mass.: Harvard University Press, 1985), 177.

6. Williams advances at least two main arguments against blame. One is the familiar argument that we cannot blame someone without presupposing that he has exercised a kind of control over his action that is so strong that we cannot coherently imagine it (since it would involve a form of self-creation) and that is in any case ruled out by determinism. For variations on this theme, see Williams, *Ethics and the Limits of Philosophy*, chapter 10, and chapters 1, 2, 6, and 21 of his *Making Sense of Humanity* (Cambridge: Cambridge University Press, 1995). The other main argument is that because blaming someone "involves treating the person who is blamed like someone who had a reason to do the right thing but did not do it" (*Making Sense of Humanity*, 42), it rests on the dubious presupposition that people can have reasons that are entirely external to their actual desires and other motivating attitudes. Because discussing these arguments would take us far afield (though I have dealt with some aspects of the first in chapter 4), I can only say here that I don't agree either that blame requires an unattainable form of control or that we cannot have normative reasons that are external to what motivates us. For useful critical discussion of Williams's position, see Garret Cullity, "Life from the Inside," *Philosophical Books* 39 (April 1998): 91–104.

run the argument in the other direction. Instead of moving from the premise that we must reject blame to the conclusion that we must reject morality, I want to move from the premise that we have good reason to embrace morality to the conclusion that we also have good reason to blame.

III

Philosophers disagree both about what morality requires and about how its requirements are to be justified. Utilitarians, Kantians, contractarians, pluralists, and others offer competing answers to both questions. However, at a more abstract level, there is considerable agreement about what morality is. There is, for example, wide agreement that the primary task of morality is to guide action; that moral principles apply at all times and places and to all persons; that moral requirements take precedence over most if not all others; and that those requirements are inescapable in the sense that we cannot choose whether or not to be bound by them.[7] Although which moral requirements really are overriding and inescapable will, of course, depend on which moral principles really are defensible, overridingness and inescapability remain formal features of morality in the sense that all putative moral principles must at least lay claim to them.

Most moral theorists agree that morality is practical, universal, omnitemporal, and (in the specified sense) overriding and inescapable. For this reason, we will beg few questions if we base our account of what is involved in accepting a moral principle exclusively on these formal features.[8] Moreover, when we consider the formal features as a

7. As is to be expected, different philosophers have stressed different entries on this list. For two discussions that together encompass all five entries, see Alan Gewirth, "The 'Is-Ought' Problem Resolved," *Proceedings and Addresses of the American Philosophical Association* XLVII (1973–74): 34–61, and R. M. Hare, *Freedom and Reason* (Oxford: Oxford University Press, 1963).

8. Our argument would not be purely formal if it took the facts that morality is practical, universal, omnitemporal, and the rest to imply the existence of a moral principle that calls upon us to have a blame-constituting desire whenever we know that someone has ignored or flouted, or is disposed to ignore or flout, one of morality's other principles. That

collectivity, we find that they do rule out the possibility of fully accepting a moral principle without wanting those who have ignored or
flouted its requirements not to have done so and those who are disposed
to ignore or flout its requirements not to be so disposed. The formal
features of morality rule this out not by establishing that it is *psycho-
logically impossible* to accept a moral principle without wanting its past
and present demands not to have gone unmet, but rather by implying
that the full acceptance of such a principle *entails or is conceptually
bound up with* having such desires. What they show, in other words, is
not that there is anything about human nature that prevents us from
accepting moral principles without having blame-constituting desires
(although it is possible that something of this sort may also be true), but
rather that any principle whose full acceptance was not accompanied by
such desires would for that very reason not qualify as moral.[9]

To see why this is so, consider first the fact that all moral principles
are practical—that their primary task is not to pass judgment on actions,
but rather to guide them. From this simple fact, we can infer that anyone
who fully accepts a given moral principle must have at least some desire

---

this argument would smuggle in substantive content is evident from the fact that utilitarianism has the formal features described in its premise, yet imposes a requirement that
is inconsistent with its conclusion. What the principle of utility requires is not that we
always want those who have failed to maximize utility to have acted differently, but rather
that we want such persons to have acted differently when, but only when, our wanting
this will itself maximize utility. Because utilitarianism is no less practical, universal,
omnitemporal, overriding, and inescapable than any other reconstruction of morality, it
is evidently possible for a coherent moral scheme to have all of these formal features
without requiring that we have a blame-constituting desire whenever one of its (other)
requirements has not been met.

9. Compare, in this regard, Scanlon's claim that "a rational person who judges there to
be a compelling reason to do A normally forms the intention to do A, and this judgment is
sufficient explanation of that intention and of the agent's acting on it" (Scanlon, *What We
Owe to Each Other*, 33–34). Like my own claim that no one can fully accept a moral
principle without wanting it not to have been violated, Scanlon's claim can be interpreted
to mean either that a certain feature of human beings (their rationality) provides a contingent psychological explanation of why they do certain things (i.e., act on the reasons they
take themselves to have), or else that it is a conceptual truth that anyone who did not act on
the reasons he took himself to have would thereby not be acting rationally.

to do what it says; for anyone who agreed that it would be wrong to act in a certain way yet had no aversion at all to doing so would clearly not be guided by whatever principle he took to be applicable. Even if he believed the principle was in some sense true, his lack of motivation to act on it would show that he did not accept it as action-guiding *for him*.

Because all desires to do things are both oriented to the future and directed exclusively at actions that we ourselves can perform, this first formal feature of morality does not by itself establish that anyone who fully accepts a moral principle must have the sorts of non-future-oriented and (often) other-directed desires that are constitutive of blame. However, it does take us some distance in that direction by establishing a conceptual connection between accepting moral principles and having certain related desires.

Bearing this connection in mind, let us next consider the fact that all moral principles are universal—that if a moral principle applies to anyone, then it applies to everyone else who is similarly situated. From this feature of morality, we clearly can infer that anyone who fully accepts a moral principle must view it as binding on others as well as himself. This is just as true, and is true for just the same reasons, as the more commonly made claim that anyone who fully accepts a moral principle must view it as binding on himself as well as others. The harder question, though, is what a moral principle's universality implies about what someone who fully accepts it must *want*. In particular, from the fact that a moral principle is universal as well as practical, can we infer that anyone who fully accepts it must want not only to obey it himself, but also that all others obey it too?

At first glance, the latter inference may seem dubious; for even if we do view a practical principle as binding on others as well as ourselves, our wanting the others to obey it is not related to their motivation as our own wanting to obey it is related to ours. When we want to obey a principle, our desire provides us with (at least some) motivation to do so; but when we want others to obey it, our desire does not similarly motivate them. (For present purposes, we may ignore the possibility that our desire that others obey the principle may indirectly motivate them by motivating us to take steps to influence their desires.) Because a desire that another person obey a moral principle is motivationally inert, it may seem possible fully to accept such a principle without having any such desires.

To say this, however, would be to misunderstand the rationale for even the uncontroversial claim that anyone who fully accepts a moral principle must want to obey it himself. Properly understood, our rationale for saying this has nothing to do with the fact that a person's wanting to obey a principle provides him with motivation *to* obey it. Instead, the point is simply that because all moral principles are prescriptive, anyone who fully accepts such a principle must have a favorable attitude toward whichever actions it prescribes. When someone can perform one of those actions himself, his favorable attitude can take the form of a desire to perform it, but when he cannot, it must take some different (though related) form. Obviously enough, the favorable attitude that is most closely related to a desire to perform a prescribed act is a desire that it *be* performed. Thus, given that all moral principles apply to all persons, we may indeed conclude that whenever someone accepts a principle as moral (as opposed, say, to embracing it simply as a personal maxim of conduct), he must have not only a motivationally effective desire to obey it himself, but also a variety of motivationally ineffective desires that others obey it as well.

In reaching this conclusion, we have moved considerably closer to the view that anyone who is fully committed to morality must have the sorts of desires that are constitutive of blame. However, because the desires discussed so far are all forward-looking, there remains a gap between them and the desires that we have when we blame people. Because the main remaining issue concerns time, the natural next step is to invoke the formal feature of morality that I have called its omnitemporality.

As we have seen, the demands of morality apply at all times as well as to all persons. If a given moral principle now demands that everyone in circumstance C perform action A, then it must also have demanded this at every moment in the past. The latter demands, though made in the past, were made by the very principle whose current acceptance is in question. Hence, as long as someone wants all of that principle's demands to be met—and, as we just saw, anyone who fully accepts a moral principle must want just this—his desires must extend backward to the past as well as outward to other people. Just as we do not fully accept a moral principle unless our motivationally effective desire to obey it is accompanied by a motivationally ineffective desire that others do so as well, we also do not fully accept a moral principle unless our motivationally mixed desires that we and others obey it now are accompanied by motivationally ineffective desires that we and they have obeyed it in the past.

When a desire that someone have obeyed a moral principle is combined with a belief that he did not do so, the result is a desire that looks a lot like some of those by which blame is constituted. Thus, we are evidently closing in on the conclusion that anyone who fully accepts a moral principle must react to wrongdoing and vice by having the relevant blame-constituting desires. However, for two reasons, we are not there yet. For one thing, because the argument so far shows only that anyone who fully accepts a moral principle must want those who have violated its requirements not to have done so, we have not yet seen why he must also want those who have the corresponding vice not to have it. In addition, because I have not said anything about the strength of the desires that must accompany the acceptance of a moral principle, it is not yet clear why those desires must be strong enough to give rise to the anger, hostile behavior, and so on, that the blame-constituting desires were introduced to explain. Thus, to complete my argument, I must now show that being fully committed to a moral principle means having desires that match the ones that are constitutive of blame in both scope and strength.

The first half of this task—showing that fully accepting a moral principle means having desires that extend to bad traits as well as bad acts—requires no additional deployment of resources. When we say that someone has a bad trait such as cruelty or dishonesty, we are saying, among other things, that that person would act cruelly or dishonestly under a broad range of conditions. These cruel and dishonest acts, if the person were to perform them, would violate whatever moral principle forbids cruelty or dishonesty. Because of this, anyone who fully accepts that principle must want the person not to perform them. Moreover, because the principle applies even to situations that will never be actualized—if it were not open-ended in this way, it would not be practical—this desire must itself have a counterfactual dimension. In addition to wanting the person not to have actually done anything cruel or dishonest, those who have the desire must want it to be the case that that he would not act cruelly or dishonestly under any alternative conditions. However, if the person were not disposed to act cruelly or dishonestly in an appropriately broad range of conditions, then he would simply not *be* cruel or dishonest. Thus, because the absence of such dispositions is part of what must be wanted, it follows that anyone who fully accepts a moral principle must indeed want those with the corresponding vice not to have it.

That brings us, finally, to the question of how strong any of these desires must be. This question is important because no mere wistful yearning could account for the vehemence and persistence of the reactions by which we manifest blame. To explain why we tend to get mad at those we blame, why we often go out of our way to reprimand them, and so on, our blame-constituting desires must be quite strong. Hence, to show that anyone who is fully committed to morality must have blame-constituting desires, I will have to show not only that his desires must have the right content, but also that they must have the right degree of strength.

There is, as far as I can see, no way to re-invoke the formal features of morality to which I have already appealed—its practicality, universality, and omnitemporality—to show that anyone who accepts a moral principle must have desires that are strong enough to be blame-constituting. However, the other two features of morality that I mentioned—its overridingness and inescapability—seem better suited to this task. As we have seen, each moral principle imposes demands that are independent of our choices and that purport to outweigh (just about) all others. Thus, to obey a moral principle consistently, we must sometimes refrain from doing what we would otherwise be inclined to do. When the desires that must be resisted are strong, our motivation to resist them must be strong as well. Hence, anyone who is committed enough to a moral principle to obey it consistently must not only have some inclination to obey it, but must care enough about doing so to be able to withstand or suppress many competing desires.[10]

Although this argument shows that anyone who is fully committed to a moral principle must have a strong desire to obey it himself, it may not seem to rule out the possibility that his desires that others obey the principle, or that he himself have done so in the past, might be much weaker. This asymmetry, if it existed, would be damaging because it would block the conclusion that being fully committed to a moral principle means having desires that support the full range of blame-constituting dispositions. However, in fact, the asymmetry *cannot* exist; for the possibility that someone who was fully committed to a moral

---

10. For interesting discussion of the fact that caring about morality comes in degrees, see Nomy Arpaly, *Unprincipled Virtue* (Oxford: Oxford University Press, 2002), 84–93.

principle could care less about disobedience by some persons than by others, or about disobedience at some times than at others, is ruled out by variants of our previous appeals to morality's universality and omnitemporality. Just as someone who wants to obey a principle without caring whether others do so is accepting it only as a personal maxim but not as a moral requirement, so too, albeit to a lesser extent, is someone who cares far *more* about his own obedience than about the obedience of others. *Mutatis mutandis*, something similar is true of a person who cares much more about obeying a principle now than about whether he or others have obeyed it in the past. Thus, when we consider all of morality's formal features together, we find that fully accepting a moral principle does require having past- and present-oriented desires that are strong enough to count as blame-constituting.[11]

IV

And because it does, we are now in a position to specify the norms that render blame-constituting desires appropriate. I have just argued that

11. Because the argument of this section turns on the assumption that moral principles are, among other things, universal, categorical, and overriding, it may seem vulnerable to the well-known arguments that virtue theorists and particularists have advanced against such principles; for some examples, see Lawrence Blum, *Friendship, Altruism, and Morality* (London: Routledge and Kegan Paul, 1980); Philippa Foot, "Morality as a System of Hypothetical Imperatives," in her *Virtues and Vices* (Berkeley: University of California Press, 1978), 157–73; and Susan Wolf, "Moral Saints," *The Journal of Philosophy* LXXIX (August 1982): 419–39. It seems to me, however, that the real target of these arguments is not the adequacy of this conception of morality but rather the view that we always ought to conform to the requirements of morality so conceived. If I am right about this, then the virtue-theoretic challenge will have no impact on my claim that anyone who fully accepts a set of moral principles is thereby committed to blaming those whom he takes to have violated them or to be disposed to do so. Moreover, even if the disagreement is over what morality is, the challenge will have no impact on the alternative version of my claim that states that anyone who fully accepts a set of principles *with the formal features that are standardly associated with morality* is thereby committed to blaming those whom he takes to have violated or to be disposed to violate those principles. Whether it is possible to defend a similar but weaker claim about someone who fully accepts a set of principles that has only some of these formal features will depend on just which deletions are envisioned.

there is a conceptual connection between fully accepting a moral principle and having blame-constituting desires when we think people have violated, or are disposed to violate, its requirements. Given this linkage, we may safely infer that anything that justifies us in accepting a moral principle must also justify us in having the corresponding blame-constituting desires. Thus, as long as there are some moral principles that we are in fact justified in accepting, there must also be some blame-constituting desires that we are justified in having. And, because of this, the obvious answer to the question of what makes a blame-constituting desire appropriate is simply that it is rendered appropriate by the same considerations—whatever these are—that justify us in accepting the moral principle whose violation, or the disposition to violate which, gives rise to it.

Bearing this answer in mind, let us return to blame itself. At the beginning of the chapter, I said that I wanted to show that there are norms that render it appropriate to react to wrongdoers and bad people in just the ways that add up to blame. That aim has now been achieved. I have argued, first, that a belief that someone has acted badly or has a bad character is rendered appropriate by the fact that the person's bad behavior or character renders it true, and, second, that a desire that someone not have acted badly or not have a bad character is rendered appropriate by the fact that it is directed at the non-occurrence of a past violation of, or the non-existence of a present disposition to violate, a moral principle that we are justified in accepting. Thus, the norms that render it appropriate to have the desire-belief combinations that I have said add up to blame stand revealed as those that require that we believe propositions that are true and that we accept moral principles that are justified.

Do these norms also explain why blame is *deserved*? Do they explain not only why it is appropriate to blame wrongdoers and bad people, but also why blame is something of which those individuals are worthy? At first glance, the norms may not seem to explain this, since what they demand is not that wrongdoers or bad people be treated in any particular ways, but only that other people (or the wrongdoers and bad people themselves in another capacity) have certain beliefs and desires whose propositional objects refer essentially to them. Because the norms are addressed to potential blamers rather than to potential blamees, their demands may seem ill-suited to support a reconstruction of what the latter agents deserve.

However, on closer inspection, there is no real problem here; for although it is true that the norms address their demands only to potential blamers, it is also true that their demands are driven by the moral quality of what the potential blamees have done or are. To satisfy those demands, a potential blamer must have the beliefs and desires that add up to blame *when and because a potential blamee has ignored or flouted, or is disposed to ignore or flout, a justified moral principle.* Because the demands that the norms address to potential blamers are thus made applicable by the badness of the acts or traits of the potential blamees, there is nothing inaccurate about saying that the reactions for which they call are precisely the ones that the potential blamees deserve. As long as it is just the badness of someone's behavior or character that renders a blame-constituting desire-belief pair appropriate, we can with equal justice describe the situation either as one in which it is appropriate for others to blame him or as one in which being blamed by others is something of which he is worthy.

Even by itself, this rejoinder would effectively block the objection that the cited norms are addressed too exclusively to potential blamers to explain how their blame can be deserved. However, the rejoinder becomes more forceful yet when we conjoin it with a thesis that was defended earlier. The thesis I have in mind is that whenever someone acts badly or has a bad trait, the features of his act or trait that make it bad can be traced to the interaction of the complex set of desires, beliefs, and fine-grained dispositions that together make him the person he is. This thesis is relevant to our current topic because it brings out just how closely the bad acts and traits that render the blame-constituting responses appropriate are linked to the characters of the agents who perform or have them. By reminding ourselves of the intimacy of this connection, we further reinforce the conclusion that any desire-belief pair that is appropriate to the badness of a person's behavior or character is for that very reason deserved by the person himself.

Can we therefore say that to be blameworthy just is to be appropriately blamed? Not quite, since a person can be blameworthy even if no one actually blames him. Someone who has acted badly may escape blame either because no one is aware of his misdeeds or because those who are aware of his misdeeds do not fully accept whatever moral principles he has ignored or flouted. *Mutatis mutandis,* the same is true of someone with a bad character. This does not mean that we cannot understand blameworthiness in terms of the appropriateness of the relevant beliefs and desires, but it does mean that we must articulate our proposal in a way that does not imply that the appropriate beliefs and desires must actually exist.

The obvious way to do this is move to a hypothetical formulation. Instead of saying that what renders someone blameworthy is the existence of a person who actually has a blame-constituting desire-belief pair whose members are rendered appropriate by the badness of his behavior or character, we must say that what renders someone blameworthy is the fact that such a desire-belief pair would be appropriate if anyone were to have it. A bit more specifically, we must say, of an agent who has acted badly, that what renders him blameworthy is the combination of the facts that

> (a) if anyone were to believe that he had ignored or flouted a justified moral principle, then that person's belief would be true, and (b) if anyone were to want him *not* to have ignored or flouted that moral principle, then that person's desire would be justified by the same considerations that would justify the person in accepting the ignored or flouted principle itself.[12]

Correspondingly, we must say of someone who has a bad trait that what renders him blameworthy is the combination of the facts that

> (a′) if anyone were to believe that he is broadly disposed to ignore or flout a justified moral principle, then that person's belief would be true, and (b′) if anyone were to want him not to be disposed to ignore or flout that moral principle, then that person's desire would be justified by the same considerations that would justify the person in accepting the relevant principle itself.

12. This account implies that whether someone is blameworthy depends not on whether he *believes* his act to be wrong, but only on whether it *is*. For an account that implies that whether someone is blameworthy depends not on whether his act is in fact wrong but only on whether he believes that it is, see Ishtiyaque Haji, *Moral Appraisability: Puzzles, Proposals, and Perplexities* (Oxford: Oxford University Press, 1998).

By shifting to these explicitly hypothetical formulations, we eliminate the final obstacle to the conclusion that blame as understood here is something of which a wrongdoer or a bad person can be worthy.

V

This account of blameworthiness is purely analytical. It tells us what blameworthiness is, but not which individuals are blameworthy—what the concept involves, but not when it is instanced. Indeed, someone could accept everything I have said about why blame-constituting beliefs and desires are appropriate reactions to the flouting or ignoring of justified moral principles, yet could also insist, with the incompatibilist, that no one ever exercises enough control over his decisions to count as having ignored or flouted, or as being disposed to ignore or flout, whichever moral principles *are* justified.

This neutrality about matters of substance is all to the good. It is good that my reconstruction of blameworthiness does not prejudge the question of who is blameworthy because the concept of blameworthiness is not the exclusive property of any single moral theory. Utilitarians, Kantians, and adherents of many other theories can all coherently say that those who violate their principles deserve to be blamed for it. For this reason, no account of blameworthiness that favored any of these theories to the exclusion of the others could possibly be adequate. Nor, for similar reasons, could any account of blameworthiness be adequate if it implied that anyone actually was blameworthy; for any account that had this implication would beg the question against the hard determinist who believes that universal causation precludes blameworthiness. By allowing the question of whether anyone is blameworthy to turn on the further question of whether anyone has ignored or flouted, or is disposed to ignore or flout, the practical reasons that justified moral principles provide, we correctly locate the dispute between hard and soft determinists in a deeper disagreement about whether universal causation undermines our ability to engage with those reasons in the requisite way.

Because my account leaves this last question open, it is not, in the strongest sense, a defense of blame. However, if we were to reject blame on the grounds that no one is ever reason-responsive, then our reason (!) for rejecting it would also be a reason to reject much else. If we did not regard ourselves as capable of recognizing and responding to reasons, it is hard to see how we could go on weighing the evidence for and against competing propositions, trying to decide what we should do, or offering moral or prudential advice to others. Although it is unclear that we could really refrain from doing these things, what does seem clear is that any such change would alter our lives in unimaginable and far-reaching ways. Thus, if we took seriously the claim that determinism undermines reason-responsiveness, the resulting inability to blame (those whom we could no longer regard as) wrongdoers or bad people would be the least of our worries.

Moreover, as long as we do not deny that agents are reason-responsive, my account does provide material for a defense of blame. Such a defense, indeed, is implicit in the argument of the two previous sections. There I argued that because accepting a moral principle is conceptually bound up with wanting its demands not to have been flouted, it follows that any considerations that justify us in accepting a moral principle must also justify us in having blame-constituting desires whenever its demands *have* been flouted. My original aim in mounting this argument was to isolate the norms that underwrite particular judgments of blameworthiness. Now, however, I want to re-invoke the argument with the larger aim of bringing out the true cost of trying to live a moral life while refusing to blame those who do not.

Put most simply, that cost would consist not of any diminution of our happiness or prosperity, but rather of our falling in a category that is disturbingly close to that of the wrongdoers and bad people whom we would refuse to blame. Like the person who does not even act on whichever moral principles are justified, the person who does act on those principles but does not care if their demands have been flouted or ignored in the past, or if anyone is disposed to flout or ignore them now, is *ipso facto* not as committed to them as their justification warrants. Even if his failure to form blame-constituting desires has no impact on the quality of his experience, there will remain a gap between the way he lives and the way he has reason to live. Thus, the price we would pay for abandoning blame is to become significantly less responsive to whichever deeper considerations provide the moral principles that we accept with their grounding.

Just how high that price is, and whether we can afford to pay it, are not questions that can be answered here. Before we could answer them, we would have to confront such difficult issues as the relations between well-being and reason-responsiveness and between an agent's normative reasons and his desires—issues that are obviously beyond our scope. However, because precisely the same issues become central when we ask why we should not act wrongly when we can get away with it, what the argument does show is that the costs of not living as morality requires and of not blaming are essentially on a par. Because the question "why blame?" is already implicit in the more familiar "why be moral?", we may conclude that Williams is right to affirm, and Pereboom therefore wrong to deny, that our reasons for acting morally and for condemning those who do not are indissolubly linked. In the end, the cases for living as morality requires and for blaming those who do not must stand or fall together.

VI

Blame can often be discerned in the interstices of the attitudes and actions of those who officially eschew it. We see this when members of the therapeutic community let slip the mask of neutrality by adopting condemnatory labels for behavior of which they disapprove; when feminists who espouse a non-judgmental "ethic of care" revert to the male-bashing of their fiercer predecessors; and when earnest efforts at reconciliation dissolve repeatedly into recriminations. We see it in even more dramatic form when those who maintain that blame is counter-productive or morally indefensible are themselves drawn to the stance of blaming (other) blamers.

Because the impulse to blame is so persistent, there are psychological as well as normative impediments to its abolition. Of course, if the reason blame is so persistent were simply that most people are inchoately aware of its connection to morality, then the psychological difficulty of avoiding it would add little to what has already been said. However, because each blame-constituting desire has a complex temporal structure—because the most important of those desires are directed at the non-existence of past decisions that when made were themselves forward-looking—their persistence may also have at least two other sources.

First, anyone who combined a future-oriented commitment to morality with an indifference to past transgressions would have a perpetually unstable set of desires. If someone wanted people to do the right thing from now on but did not care whether they had done the right thing in the past, then what he cared about would be constantly changing. As each moment slipped from the future into the past, he would have to relinquish his desire that he and other people do the right thing at that moment. Such systematic shifts in our attitudes are not unheard of—as Derek Parfit has noted, our attitudes toward our own suffering appear to shift in just this way[13]—but neither are they the norm. Often our desires do survive changes in tense, as when we move effortlessly from wanting our candidate to win the election to wanting him to have won it. Thus, blame's persistence may in part be due to pressure to keep our desires consistent over time. Alternatively or in addition, it may simply reflect a form of attitudinal inertia.[14]

And the persistence of blame may draw also support from another quarter: namely, the fact that thinking of someone as having ignored or flouted a moral reason often involves entering imaginatively into that person's earlier deliberative perspective. Speaking of the potential blamee as the defendant and the potential blamer as the judge, Thomas Nagel has described the phenomenon this way:

> [I]n a judgment of responsibility the judge doesn't just decide that what has been done is a good or a bad thing, but tries to enter into the defendant's point of view as an agent. . . . he tries to assess the action in light of the alternatives presenting themselves to the defendant—among which he chose or failed to choose, and in light of the considerations and temptations bearing on that choice—which he considered or failed to consider.[15]

When we identify in this manner with someone whom we take to have acted badly, we imagine ourselves as confronting the options that

---

13. See Derek Parfit, *Reasons and Persons* (Oxford: Oxford University Press, 1984), chap. 8.

14. For related discussion, see my *Desert* (Princeton, N.J.: Princeton University Press, 1987), chap. 10.

15. Thomas Nagel, *The View from Nowhere* (Oxford: Oxford University Press, 1986), 120.

he took himself to confront and we imagine the choice among those options as not yet made. By thus imaginatively collapsing both the temporal and the personal distance between the agent and ourselves, we think of his options as ones to which our own future-oriented moral commitments apply. Hence, when those commitments call for a choice that is different from his, it is only to be expected that our identification with him will lead us to want him to have made that choice.

Here, then, are several distinct intellectual pressures that seem to push us in the direction of wanting those whom we take to have acted badly not to have done so (and, though probably to a lesser degree, in the direction of wanting those whom we take to be disposed to act badly not to be so disposed). To the extent that these pressures are strong, abandoning blame will not be an easy matter; to the extent that they are too strong to resist on a regular basis, there will be a psychological as well as a normative sense in which blame and a commitment to morality must stand or fall together.

Is there then nothing to be said for the idea that we would all be better off if we simply let bygones be bygones? Not necessarily, since there is more to blame than the relevant desire-belief pairs. As we saw in the previous chapter, each blame-constituting desire-belief pair standardly gives rise to a characteristic set of behavioral and affective dispositions. Because the relation between the desire-belief pairs and the dispositions is merely contingent,[16] it would not be inconsistent for someone to acknowledge both the moral importance and the unavoidability of the desire-belief pairs but to deny either the moral importance or the unavoidability of the dispositions to which they standardly give rise. Thus, despite the fact that being fully committed to morality requires that we have blame-constituting desires whenever we have the corresponding beliefs, we cannot automatically infer that it also requires the rancor and recriminations with which blame is

---

16. The contingency of the connection between the desire-belief pairs and the dispositions does not conflict with my earlier claim that we might not be willing to describe a person as blaming someone unless he had them both. It is perfectly possible for a single concept to require the presence of two or more contingently related factors: think of the concept "table," which applies only to things that have both legs and a flat surface.

commonly associated. Because my account of blame is two-tiered, we may legitimately ask how far into the second tier the requirements of a commitment to morality extend.

I think the answer to this question is not clear. The reason for its unclarity is not that there is room for disagreement about whether the dispositions to become angry at wrongdoers and bad people, to reproach them, and so on are among the logically necessary conditions for blaming; for even if these dispositions *are* part of what we mean when we speak of blame, it will remain possible to introduce a more stripped-down notion which takes blaming to consist exclusively of having the relevant desires and beliefs. Instead, the important unresolved issues are, first, whether it is realistically possible to make the transition to blaming people only in this more stripped-down way, and, second, whether such a change, assuming it to be possible, would make our lives better.

As I have said, I am not sure what the answers to these questions are. On the one hand, even though our dispositions to react to those whom we view as wrongdoers and bad people with anger, hostility, reproach, and the rest are only contingently connected to our blame-constituting desires, they may be no less deeply rooted in our psychology than are those desires themselves. Also, as utilitarians often remind us, it is precisely the unpleasantness of the anger and reproaches that wrongdoers and bad people must often endure that allows those reactions to play their valuable educative and deterrent role. However, on the other hand, it may be possible to improve the quality of our social relations by lowering the condemnatory volume and compensating for any resulting diminution of social control in other ways. It is one thing to say that living a fully moral life requires blaming those who ignore or flout morality's demands, but quite another to say that it requires the kind of toxic anger that makes future harmony more difficult to achieve. That we would be better off if we were to weaken the connection between blame and rancor may be the kernel of truth in the anti-blame ideology, but that we would be better off if we abandoned blame itself is the larger falsehood in which that kernel is embedded.

BIBLIOGRAPHY

Adams, Robert Merrihew. "Involuntary Sins." *The Philosophical Review* XCIV (January 1985): 3–31.

———. *Finite and Infinite Goods: A Framework for Ethics.* Oxford: Oxford University Press, 1999.

Arneson, Richard. "The Smart Theory of Moral Responsibility and Desert." In *Desert and Justice,* edited by Serena Olsaretti, 233–63. Oxford: Oxford University Press, 2003.

Arpaly, Nomy. *Unprincipled Virtue.* Oxford: Oxford University Press, 2002.

Arpaly, Nomy, and Timothy Schroeder. "Praise, Blame, and the Whole Self." *Philosophical Studies* 93 (February 1999): 162–88.

Baron, Marcia. *Kantian Ethics Almost Without Apology.* Ithaca, N.Y.: Cornell University Press, 1995.

Bennett, Jonathan. "Accountability." In *Philosophical Subjects: Essays Presented to P. F. Strawson,* edited by Zak Van Straaten. Oxford: Oxford University Press, 1980.

Blum, Lawrence. *Friendship, Altruism, and Morality.* London: Routledge and Kegan Paul, 1980.

———. *Moral Perception and Particularity.* Cambridge: Cambridge University Press, 1994.

Brandt, Richard. "Blameworthiness and Obligation." In *Essays in Moral Psychology,* edited by A. I. Melden, 3–39. Seattle: University of Washington Press, 1958.

Campbell, C. A. *In Defense of Free Will.* London: George Allen and Unwin, 1967.

Chisholm, Roderick. "Human Freedom and the Self," in *Reason at Work: Introductory Readings in Philosophy,* 3rd ed., edited by Steven M. Cahn, Patricia Kitcher, George Sher, and Peter Markie, 536–46. Fort Worth, Tex.: Harcourt Brace, 1996.

Cullity, Garret. "Life from the Inside." *Philosophical Books* 39 (April 1998): 91–104.

Dancy, Jonathan. *Moral Reasons*. Oxford: Blackwell, 1993.

Doris, John. *Lack of Character*. Cambridge: Cambridge University Press, 2002.

Ellis, Albert, and Robert A. Harper. *A Guide for Rational Living*, 3rd ed. North Hollywood, Calif.: Wilshire Book Company, 1997.

Fischer, John Martin ed. *Moral Responsibility*. Ithaca, NY: Cornell University Press, 1986.

Foot, Philippa. *Virtues and Vices*. Berkeley: University of California Press, 1978.

Frankfurt, Harry. *The Importance of What We Care About*. Cambridge: Cambridge University Press, 1988.

Gewirth, Alan. "The 'Is-Ought' Problem Resolved." *Proceedings and Addresses of the American Philosophical Association* XLVII (1973–74): 34–61.

Gibbard, Allan. *Wise Feelings, Apt Choices*. Cambridge, Mass.: Harvard University Press, 1990.

Glover, Jonathan. *Responsibility*. London: Routledge and Kegan Paul, 1970.

Haji, Ishtiyaque. *Moral Appraisability: Puzzles, Proposals, and Perplexities*. Oxford: Oxford University Press, 1998.

Hare, R. M. *Freedom and Reason*. Oxford: Oxford University Press, 1963.

Harman, Gilbert. "Moral Psychology Meets Social Psychology: Virtue Ethics and the Fundamental Attribution Error." *Proceedings of the Aristotelian Society, New Series* XCIX, part 3 (1999): 315–51.

Hegel, G. W. F. *The Philosophy of Right*. Translated by F. M. Knox. Oxford: Oxford University Press, 1942.

Hill, Thomas. *Dignity and Practical Reason in Kant's Moral Theory*. Ithaca, N.Y.: Cornell University Press, 1992.

Hobart, R. E. "Free Will as Involving Determination and Inconceivable Without It." In *Free Will and Determinism*, ed. Bernard Berofsky, 63–95. New York: Harper and Row, 1966.

Honderich, Ted. *A Theory of Determinism: The Mind, Neuroscience, and Life-Hopes*. Oxford: Oxford University Press, 1998.

Hume, David. *An Inquiry Concerning Human Understanding*. Edited by Charles W. Hendel. Indianapolis, Ind.: Bobbs-Merrill, 1955.

———. *A Treatise of Human Nature*. Edited by L. A. Selby-Bigge. Oxford: Oxford University Press, 1960.

Kant, Immanuel. *The Philosophy of Law, Part II*. Translated by W. Hastie. In *Philosophical Perspectives on Punishment*, edited by Gertrude Ezorsky, 103–06. Albany: State University of New York Press, 1972.

Kupperman, Joel. *Character*. New York: Oxford University Press, 1991.

Locke, John. *An Essay Concerning Human Understanding*. Edited by Alexander Campbell Fraser. New York: Dover, 1959.

Louden, Robert B. "On Some Vices of Virtue Ethics." In *Virtue Ethics*, edited by Roger Crisp and Michael Slote, 201–16. Oxford: Oxford University Press, 1997.

McDowell, John. "Are Moral Requirements Hypothetical Imperatives?" *Proceedings of the Aristotelian Society* (1978, supplementary volume): 13–29.

————. "Virtue and Reason." In *Virtue Ethics*, edited by Roger Crisp and Michael Slote, 141–62. Oxford: Oxford University Press, 1997.

Milgram, Stanley. *Obedience to Authority*. New York: Harper and Row, 1974.

Milo, Ronald. *Immorality*. Princeton, N.J.: Princeton University Press, 1984.

Moody-Adams, Michele. "On the Old Saw That Character Is Destiny." In *Identify, Character, and Morality*, edited by Owen Flanagan and Amelie Oksenberg Rorty, 111–31. Cambridge, Mass.: MIT Press, 1990.

Moore, Michael. *Placing Blame*. Oxford: Oxford University Press, 1997.

Morris, Herbert. *On Guilt and Innocence*. Berkeley and Los Angeles: University of California Press, 1976.

Murphy, Jeffrie G. and Jean Hampton. *Forgiveness and Mercy*. Cambridge: Cambridge University Press, 1988.

Nagel, Thomas. *The Possibility of Altruism*. Oxford: Oxford University Press, 1970.

————. *Mortal Questions*. Cambridge: Cambridge University Press, 1979.

————. *The View from Nowhere*. Oxford: Oxford University Press, 1986.

Nietzsche, Friedrich. *Thus Spake Zarathustra*. Translated by Walter Kaufmann. New York: Viking, 1954.

————. *On the Geneology of Morals*. Translated by Walter Kaufmann. New York: Vintage, 1969.

Nowell-Smith, P. H. *Ethics*. Baltimore: Penguin Books, 1954.

Nozick, Robert. *Philosophical Explanations*. Cambridge, Mass.: Harvard University Press, 1981.

Nussbaum, Martha. *Love's Knowledge: Essays on Philosophy and Literature*. New York: Oxford University Press, 1990.

Parfit, Derek. *Reasons and Persons*. Oxford: Oxford University Press, 1984.

Parker, Clint. "Complicity." Ph.D. diss., Rice University, 2002.

Pereboom, Derk. "Determinism Al Dente." In *Free Will*, edited by Derk Pereboom, 242–72. Indianapolis, Ind.: Hackett, 1997.

————. *Living Without Free Will*. Cambridge: Cambridge University Press, 2001.

Rawls, John. *A Theory of Justice*. Cambridge, Mass.: Harvard University Press, 1971.

Rescher, Nicholas. "Moral Luck." In *Moral Luck*, edited by Daniel Statman, 141–66. Albany: State University of New York Press, 1993.

Ryle, Gilbert. *The Concept of Mind*. New York: Barnes and Noble, 1949.

Scanlon, T. M. "The Significance of Choice." In *Equal Freedom: Selected Tanner Lectures on Human Values*, edited by Stephen Darwall, 39–104. Ann Arbor: University of Michigan Press, 1995.

————. *What We Owe to Each Other*. Cambridge, Mass.: Harvard University Press, 1998.

Schlick, Moritz. "When Is a Man Responsible?" In *Free Will and Determinism*, edited by Bernard Berofsky, 54–63. New York: Harper and Row, 1966.

Shah, Nishi. "How Truth Governs Belief." *The Philosophical Review* 112 (October 2003): 447–82.

Sher, George. *Approximate Justice: Studies in Non-Ideal Theory*. Lanham, Md.: Rowman and Littlefield, 1997.

———. *Desert*. Princeton, NJ: Princeton University Press, 1987.

———. "Kantian Fairness." *Philosophical Issues*, forthcoming.

———. "Out of Control." *Ethics*, forthcoming.

Sherman, Nancy. *The Fabric of Character*. Oxford: Oxford University Press, 1989.

Smart, J. J. C. "Free Will, Praise, and Blame." In *Determinism, Free Will, and Moral Responsibility*, edited by Gerald Dworkin, 196–213. Englewood Cliffs, N.J.: Prentice-Hall, 1970.

Smart, J. J. C., and Bernard Williams. *Utilitarianism: For and Against*. Cambridge: Cambridge University Press, 1973.

Smith, Michael. *The Moral Problem*. Oxford: Blackwell, 1994.

Strawson, P. F. "Freedom and Resentment." In *Free Will*, edited by Derk Pereboom, 119–42. Indianapolis, Ind.: Hackett, 1997.

Velleman, David. *The Possibility of Practical Reason*. Oxford: Oxford University Press, 2000.

Wallace, James. *Virtues and Vices*. Ithaca, N.Y.: Cornell University Press, 1978.

Wallace, R. Jay. "How to Argue About Practical Reason." *Mind* XCIX (July 1990): 355–85.

———. *Responsibility and the Moral Sentiments*. Cambridge, Mass.: Harvard University Press, 1994.

Watson, Gary. "Free Agency." *The Journal of Philosophy* 72 (April 24, 1975): 205–20.

———. "Responsibility and the Limits of Evil." In *Responsibility, Character, and the Emotions: New Essays in Moral Psychology*, edited by Ferdinand Schoeman, 256–86. Cambridge: Cambridge University Press, 1987.

Wertheimer, Roger. "Constraining Condemning." *Ethics* 108 (April 1998):489–501.

Williams, Bernard. *Ethics and the Limits of Philosophy*. Cambridge, Mass.: Harvard University Press, 1985.

———. *Making Sense of Humanity and Other Philosophical Papers*. Cambridge: Cambridge University Press, 1995.

———. *Truth and Truthfulness*. Princeton, N.J.: Princeton University Press, 2002.

Wolf, Susan. "Moral Saints." *The Journal of Philosophy* LXXIX (August 1982): 419–39.

———. *Freedom Within Reason*. New York: Oxford University Press, 1990.

Zimmerman, Michael. *An Essay on Moral Responsibility*. Totowa, N.J.: Rowman and Littlefield, 1988.

INDEX